The Gaelic Place Names and Heritage of Inverness

Roddy Maclean

Culcabock Publishing
Inverness

1

*Mar chuimhneachan air Roy Wentworth nach maireann,
sàr-Ghaidheal a dhearbh dhuinn uile na th' againn de bheartas
nar n-ainmean-àite is dualchas cànain.*

ISBN Number: 0-9548925-0-X

Published by Culcabock Publishing, Inverness
Printed by Highland Printers, Inverness

Contents

A Message from the Provost   5

Ro-ràdh   7

Introduction   11

A Short History of Gaelic in Inverness   15

Some Place Names No Longer in General Use   45

Place Names Still in Use   57

Mar a Fhuair Loch Nis ainm   89

Buidheachas   90

Bibliography   91

Index   93

The Provost of Inverness, William J Smith, outside the Town House next to one of Inverness's great Gaelic landmarks - Clach na Cùdainn *(see p. 66)*

A Message from the Provost of Inverness

It is a great honour to be Provost of Inverness, the "Capital of the Highlands", during a period of growth and change in the city, and to be asked to write this foreword. We are faced with many challenges, among which is the maintenance of the clean and beautiful environment that has served as a magnet for several thousand people from all points of the compass who have settled, or intend to settle, in Inverness.

We also face a linguistic challenge. There is a renewed interest in the Gaelic language, with the Scottish Executive requiring Bòrd na Gàidhlig, which has its headquarters in Inverness, to prepare a National Gaelic Language Plan during the term of the current parliament. With the assistance of modern technology, we may be about to see a revival of the language in our city, and Highland Council is playing its part with a proposal to build a new Gaelic Medium primary school to the south of the city, subject to Scottish Executive funding. As Roddy Maclean points out in his text, it will not be the first in the area, as Clachnaharry boasted a Gaelic school in the 19th Century, but it will be the first in the modern era and a major boost for the language nationwide.

This interesting book confirms the use of Gaelic in Inverness in the past, and provides detailed background information in support of the language. We have a saying in Gaelic – "Togar càrn mòr de chlachan beaga" – a big cairn is built from small stones. It is up to our generation to start putting the first small stones in place.

William J Smith
Provost of Inverness

5

Inverness - Inbhir Nis
The mouth of the River Ness

This view of Inverness from the north abounds in Gaelic place names, some of them very old. In the distance is Druim Aithisidh *(Drumossie) and on the right of the picture (background) is the famous hill known as* Tom na h-Iùbhraich *(Tomnahurich), close to* Dail an Eich *(Dalneigh).* Marc-Innis *(Merkinch) and* Capall-Innis *(Capel Inch) are at centre right. While we know the original forms and meanings of these names, others remain enigmatic. The sweep of the river on this side of the first bridge is called* The Cherry, *a name which might be a corruption of a Gaelic reference to the high-tide mark.* Carnarc Point *at the river mouth (centre left) is another name whose original form remains a matter for debate.*

Ro-ràdh

Bha mi a-riamh dhen bheachd gu robh ainmean-àite na Gàidhealtachd a' fosgladh doras do mhuinntir na h-Alba a bheireadh iad a dh'ionnsaigh tuigse na b' fheàrr air suidheachadh an cànain agus, nuair a ghluais mi a dh'Inbhir Nis an toiseach, thàinig e gu m' aire gu bheil sin a cheart cho fìor mun bhaile seo 's a tha e mu na monaidhean is beanntan far a bheil ainmean Gàidhlig a' lìonadh cairt na dùthcha fhathast. Anns an Eilean Sgitheanach, far an robh mi a' fuireach roimhe, buinidh cuid mhath de na h-ainmean-àite do dhualchas nan Lochlannach ach, ann an Inbhir Nis, dh'èirich a' chuid as mò aca (co-dhiù an fheadhainn nach robh air an taghadh le bàillidhean a' bhaile) bhon chànan a bu mhotha a bh' air a bruidhinn le muinntir an àite airson ùine – a' Ghàidhlig.

Ach thàinig e gu m' aire cuideachd gu robh mòran ann an Inbhir Nis aineolach mu eachdraidh a' bhaile aca, 's nach robh fios aca gu robh Gàidhlig aig mòran de na sinnsirean aca. Mar a chì sinn anns an teacs a leanas, bha iad air tighinn fo bhuaidh faoinsgeòil – gur e baile aon-chànanach na Beurla a bh' ann an Inbhir Nis fad nan linntean mòra.

O chionn grunn bhliadhnaichean, chaidh mi gu coinneamh aig seann Chomhairle Sgìre Inbhir Nis, nuair a bha ùghdarrasan ionadail na h-Alba dà-fhillte. Bha i ann an seòmar brèagha eachdraidheil Taigh a' Bhaile, agus b' e am prìomh chuspair air a' chlàr – moladh airson soidhnichean-sràide ùra ann am meadhan Inbhir Nis, a ghabhadh àite na seann fheadhainn a bha a' fàs meargach. Dè bha connspaideach mu dheidhinn sin? Bha na soidhnichean gu bhith dà-chànanach. Beurla agus Gàidhlig.

Dh'èirich aon chomhairliche gu chasan. Bha seo, thuirt e, coltach ri "Brigadoon" a dhèanamh de dh'Inbhir Nis. Nach robh fios againn uile nach robh Gàidhlig a-riamh aig muinntir a' bhaile seo? Fhuair e taic bho chuid eile. Agus chan e coigrich a bh' annta. Bhuineadh iad don Ghàidhealtachd. Bha mi ann mar fhear-naidheachd airson aithris a dhèanamh air a' choinneimh, ach bha e fìor dhoirbh dhomh mo bheul a chumail dùinte agus an fhearg a bha ag èirigh nam chridhe a cheannsachadh!

Co-dhiù, chaidh an là leis na Gaidheil agus an luchd-taic, gu h-àraidh air sgàth 's gu robh buidheann Ghàidhlig gu bhith a' pàigheadh airson nan soidhnichean ùra. Ach, ann an dòigh, bhuannaich an t-aineolas cuideachd,

7

MERKINCH

Inshes

Peat...

LOCHGORM

tapadh leibh airson
ceannach againn

Baile Beag a' Chnuic

Road to

Central Primary School
Bunsgoil a' Mheadhain
The Highland Council

INVERNE...

SLACKBUIE AVENUE

...n amhairc

LEACHKIN

E...
Balvonie
A-Mach

CREAG DHUB...

BALLIFEARY

...eachadh
toirmisgte
gun chead

SEIRBHEIS...
IS ÀRAINNEACH...
IS COIMHEARSNACHD

BALNAFETT...

INBHE
MALAI...

Na toiribh troilidhean
seachad air seo
Tapadh leibh

leis gu robh an sgrìobhadh Gàidhlig a chuireadh air na soidhnichean cho beag 's gu bheil e doirbh a leughadh.

'S e facal cruaidh a th' ann an "aineolas", ach dè eile a chanamaid? Cha robh fios aig na comhairlichean sin gu robh na mìltean thar mhìltean de luchd-còmhnaidh ann, thairis air eachdraidh fhada Inbhir Nis, aig nach robh Beurla a-riamh. Eadhon nuair a chaidh an togalach anns an robhar a' deasbad a thogail, eadar 1878 agus 1882, bha Gàidhlig aig cha mhòr duine às gach triùir de mhuinntir a' bhaile.

'S dòcha nach iad na comhairlichean fhèin a bu choireach. Bha am faoinsgeul cho cumhachdach 's gur gann gu robh cothrom aca an taobh eile a chluinntinn anns an sgoil no anns a' choimhearsnachd. Ach chan urrainn do mo leithid an gnothach fhàgail aig a sin. "Is trom an t-eallach an t-aineolas," tha an seanfhacal ag innse dhuinn, agus tha e mar uallach air Gàidheil an là an-diugh, aig a bheil gràdh do dh'Inbhir Nis, an t-eallach sin a thogail.

'S ann air an fheasgar sin ann an Taigh a' Bhaile a chuir mi romham an leabhar beag seo a sgrìobhadh, leis an amas dualchas Gàidhlig Inbhir Nis a thoirt gu aire a' mhòr-shluaigh, ged a thug e ro fhada a thoirt gu buil. Agus, às dèidh dhomh an rannsachadh airson an leabhair a chrìochnachadh ann an 2004, chaidh iarraidh orm nochdadh mu choinneimh comhairlichean Inbhir Nis airson eachdraidh na Gàidhlig anns a' bhaile a mhìneachadh dhaibh - anns an dearbh sheòmar far an cuala mi na beachdan nimheil bliadhnaichean roimhe. An turas seo bhathar a' deasbad co-dhiù chuirte dà mhìle not a dh'ionnsaigh stèidheachadh dreuchd oifigear-leasachaidh na Gàidhlig sa bhaile. Agus bha cuid de na comhairlichean a cheart cho nàimhdeil don chànan 's a bha iad a' chiad turas.

Chaidh an là leis na Gàidheil a-rithist, ach bhiodh e math nan tachradh a leithid gun strì mhòr gach turas. Co-dhiù, mo thaing do na comhairlichean ionadail a bha, agus a tha, taiceil don chànan, am Pròbhaist (aig a bheil i gu fileanta) nam measg. Mo thaing cuideachd do dh'Uilleam Mac a' Ghobhainn airson a theachdaireachd laghach a chur an cois an leabhair seo. Bidh sinn an dòchas nach esan am Pròbhaist mu dheireadh againn aig a bheil comas-labhairt anns an dà chànan a th' aig cridhe dualchas Prìomh Bhaile na Gaidhealtachd.

Ruairidh MacIlleathain
Inbhir Nis 2004

Horse fair circa 1894 on Bank Street. Horses were an important part of life in past times and three different Gaelic words for horse - marc, capall *and* each *- are found in Inverness place names (see p. 48)*

Introduction

To outsiders, it might seem obvious that Inverness, bearing a Gaelic name, and long being touted as the "Capital of the Highlands" must have a Celtic heritage of sorts. But it might also surprise them that many Invernessians have sought to distance themselves from that Gaelic past and that some have gone so far as to deny it entirely. Lord Macaulay's statement that the town, now officially a "city", was a "Saxon colony among the Celts" has been quoted more than once as a justification for that point of view. The further development of his analysis – that Inverness was a "hive of traders and artisans in the midst of a colony of loungers and plunderers, a solitary outpost of civilisation in a region of barbarism" – may have been embarrassingly partial, but it accorded with a general view that the town was a place apart, hermetically sealed, in terms of language and identity, from the Gaelic Highlands which surrounded it on all sides.

Macaulay's assessment has been too often repeated without scrutiny or scepticism. The myth which he helped to establish, and which has still not been consigned to the dustbin for flawed analyses, was that Inverness was inhabited for all its long history solely by an Anglophone people who had no truck with Celtic civilisation. And it is not only non-Gaels who have fallen prey to the myth. Kenneth MacDonald, Town Clerk of Inverness, and a man of undoubtedly Celtic background, told the Inverness Scientific Society and Field Club in March 1895 that in the 17th Century the town was, and had long been, mainly Anglo-Saxon, an English-speaking colony in the midst of Celtic and Gaelic-speaking clans.

Yet, as Mr MacDonald was addressing the club, nearly one in three Invernessians – thirty percent according to the census of 1891 – were still speaking Gaelic. They were out there in their homes and in the streets talking, arguing, trading, telling secrets, bragging, gossiping, loving and fighting in the language of the Gael. Despite this, in 1912, a paper to the Inverness Scientific Society and Field Club by an ex-President, Mr H.C. Boyd, stated that, "Inverness has always been, so far back as you can go in the written record, an English-speaking town, for the chief burgesses were Teutonic,

11

not Celtic, though there were also a great many Celts in the population." One might ask what happened to these Celts – did they simply give up their language upon first contact with the element of the town's population which did not speak Gaelic? The evidence suggests they did not. And, anyway, is the history of Inverness only the story of its civic leaders?

The myth lingered on through the twentieth century. Gerald Pollitt, in his 1981 book *Historic Inverness,* wrote that, "As far back as written records go Inverness has always been a peaceful marketing centre supporting the ruling monarch, an English-speaking town set in the midst of a Celtic and Gaelic-speaking population."

To be fair to Pollitt and others, the myth was based to a degree on accounts which had been made by travellers to Inverness. John Mackay wrote in 1717 of the excellent English spoken by Invernessians, as did Samuel Johnson following his brief sojourn in August 1773. A particularly opinionated 18th Century account was given by Daniel Defoe who, in addition to praising the "remarkably handsome" women of the town, postulated that the "perfect English" spoken in Inverness ("some will say as well as at London itself") was a result of the influence of Oliver Cromwell's soldiers who built a fort in the vicinity of the harbour.

But it appears they missed something. I am reminded of the comments of several travellers of my acquaintance from distant parts of the world who have journeyed extensively in the Western Isles in recent years. They claimed not to have heard a word of Gaelic spoken in their entire stay. Even in the most strongly Gaelic communities in the islands today, where Gaelic is overwhelmingly the language of the home (but hidden from view in that context), the newspapers are in English, the shop signs are in English, public meetings and notices are in English and no stranger will ever be addressed in Gaelic unless he or she initiates a conversation in that language. One can easily imagine a traveller in 18th Century Inverness making company with affluent English-speaking townsfolk and being all but oblivious to the language being spoken in the homes of the poor.

That can surely be the only explanation for the contradictory evidence provided by such travellers as Thomas Kirk who wrote in 1677, in reference to Gaelic, that, "all in the town in Inverness do generally use that language....." And his opinion is backed up by many more accounts. The truth of the matter is that both linguistic elements co-existed in the town for many centuries, just as they do in today's modern vibrant city. Gaelic appears to have been numerically dominant for a period of time, but that mantle has been thoroughly and increasingly adopted by English over the last two centuries. Inverness nevertheless remains a bilingual community today.

There is much evidence to support the contention that Gaelic had a significant presence in Inverness, both inside its ancient town boundaries and in the wider rural environment which has been swallowed up by rapidly expanding urban development and which lies today under the city's houses and roads. A prime source of this evidence is in the names of objects and places - not the landmarks given labels by decree of the town's burgesses but those which grew by organic processes from the mouths of the inhabitants. Scorguie, Merkinch, Inshes, Ballifeary, Dalneigh, Clachnaharry, Tomnahurich and Culcabock, for example, all originated as Gaelic names. So did *Clach na Cùdainn* (Clachnacuddin), the stone which for long represented, more powerfully than any other object, Inverness's individual identity. The obvious inference is that the people who named these places and objects spoke Gaelic.

The purpose of this book is to encourage a better understanding of Inverness's cultural heritage and, in so doing, to challenge a pernicious myth which still stalks the streets of a city that has taken upon itself the mantle of "Highland Capital". Can it be conscionable to accept such an accolade if the greatest single emblem of Highland identity – the Gaelic language – is to be denied its rightful and proper place in the city, both in today's world and in retrospect among the yellowing pages of history?

In the chapters which follow, we shall look at the probable origins and meanings of many of the place names in and around Inverness, the majority of them Gaelic in origin. That in itself is a journey of sorts, and fascinating in its own right. But first we must visit the Inverness of byegone centuries and listen to its people speak as best we can...

Kessock Ferry 1896. A ferry plied the waters connecting Inverness to the Black Isle for many centuries until the construction of the Kessock Bridge. The name Kessock derives from an early Celtic saint (see p. 79)

A Short History of Gaelic in Inverness

We shall never know when the first Gaelic-speaker cast his or her eyes upon the sparkling beauty of the River Ness, but we have reason to believe that one had dipped her feet in the cool waters of the river, or had travelled across or upon it, even before the arrival of the great Saint Columba from Iona in the middle of the 6th Century AD. Why "her"? Simply because the saint's biographer, Adamnan, the ninth abbot of Iona, tells us in his *Life of Columba* that the founder of his establishment arranged for an Irish slave-girl to be freed from the grip of Broichan, the chief magician of King Brude, upon a visit to the Pictish leader whose fortress was at, or close to, Inverness. The girl's native tongue would almost certainly have been Gaelic.

Even if Columba failed to meet the slave-girl, it is certain that he spoke to his Gaelic-speaking companions on the banks of the Ness, and we can thus date the first known Gaelic conversation on the site of Inverness to nearly fourteen and a half centuries ago. That is a substantial pedigree by anybody's reckoning.

In the centuries following Columba, the northern part of Scotland became steadily more Gaelicised. Pictish power waned, the two peoples combined under common leadership, and the Picts quietly disappeared. The Norsemen, however, with centres of power in Orkney, Shetland and the Hebrides, came into the picture in the coastal eastern Highlands. The occasional Norse place name in the general area (Dingwall being a prime example) attests to the presence of their language, although there is little today which can be identified as Norse in Inverness.

It is also possible that some of Inverness's oldest Gaelic place names date from this early period. Certainly, by the time that MacBeth came to the throne in 1040, when he is reputed to have had a castle in Inverness, the language was thriving, not only at the level of the Royal court but also within the wider population of Scotland. But the picture, at least as far as royalty is concerned, was to change dramatically in the twelfth and thirteenth centuries, with the growing influence of elements whose native or ancestral tongues were the Anglo-Saxon of Northumbria and the French of Normandy. Another linguistic element was also to enter at Inverness at this stage – the Flemish of the Low Countries.

MacBeth's castle, which was probably situated in the Crown to the east of the present town centre, was abandoned in favour of the current location, where

Saint Columba and Inverness

Adamnan's description of miracles conducted by Saint Columba in his *Vita Columbae* (Life of Columba) is the earliest written account of the Inverness area. The most famous story concerns a monster in the River Ness. When Columba and his companions reached the banks of the river, they came upon a party burying a man who had been attacked by the monster while swimming.

Columba ordered an associate, Lugne Mocumin, to swim across the river to bring him a boat from the far side. As Lugne reached the middle of the current, the monster made for him. Columba, however, made a sign of the cross in the air and, invoking the name of God, commanded the beast to "Go no further, nor touch the man; go back at once." The monster turned and fled. Even the non-Christian Picts were astounded by the miracle and "magnified the God of the Christians".

The other stories concern the struggle for spiritual supremacy between Columba and the Druid, Broichan, who had a special place in the court of the Pictish king, Brude. Broichan refused to part with an Irish slave-girl, so Columba threatened him in the presence of the king, saying that he would die if the captive were not freed. Columba then went to the banks of the River Ness and picked up a white pebble, telling his companions that the Lord would use it to effect many cures. He told them that Broichan had been smitten by an angel from heaven and that because he was dying, he would be willing to free the girl.

As Columba was speaking, two horsemen arrived from the king with confirmation of everything he had said. He sent two of his companions to the royal fortress with the magic stone and instructions as to its use and when Broichan released the slave-girl, the stone was put in water; amazingly it could not be made to sink. Broichan drank the water in which it was immersed and he immediately recovered from "imminent death".

When Columba was about to return to Iona, sailing the length of Loch Ness on the first part of his journey, Broichan told him that he would cause a contrary tempest to prevent him travelling. Columba replied that such things were only in the power of God and he prepared to sail. When the day came, a storm did indeed gather, with the wind against the sailors, causing rejoicing amongst the druids. Not to be daunted, Columba ordered the boat to be rigged and took off into the wind at great speed. Shortly after, the storm abated, the wind swung around and the voyage was conducted as the great churchman had predicted.

a collection of houses came to gather around a new fortification on Castle Hill. The town was created a Royal Burgh and, in order to ensure that it acted in the (now anglicised) monarch's favour, the king encouraged the settlement of people who would be loyal to him and disinclined to side with any rebellious Gaelic warlords in the north.

Some of the surnames from the 13th Century demonstrate the success of this policy: Blund, Noreys, Monte-alto, de Grant, de Braytoft, de la Haye and Pilchys are examples. It should be noted, however, that the de Grants, at this time Norman in character, were to become Gaelicised in time as *na Granndaich*, or Grants. And, of course, it is impossible to assess whether the "foreign" character of the noteworthy citizens of Inverness was reflected in the town's population as a whole, or whether it was a feature of only the upper echelons, whose names were recorded for posterity.

Despite undoubted control of the town by non-Gaels at this time, the place name heritage points to the presence of Gaelic. Balnafare (now Ballifeary) is recorded as early as the 13th Century. This was *Baile na Faire*, the township of the watch; while outside the old town boundary, it was a place intimately connected with the wellbeing of the town, for it was the location of watchers who would warn the townsfolk of any approaching danger from the west of the Ness. Other Gaelic place names relating directly to the life of the town also date back to these times, suggesting that the language had a significant presence, whatever its status in government might have been. And names like *Cill Bheathain* (Kilvean) and *Tòrr Bheathain* (Torvean), which relate to a figure within the early Celtic Church, are probably many centuries older than that.

The dominance of non-Gaels within the halls of power continued in the 14th Century, with names like Pilch, Vaus, Lambe, de Fotheringham and Cuthbert appearing in the town records, but by the 15th Century there was a slight but distinct shift towards a more Gaelic flavour in the personal nomenclature. This is not only true in terms of surnames or family names, one-eighth of which were now Gaelic, but in the appearance of Celtic given names as well. In addition to such as Henry and Richard, we now see Donald, Duncan, Dugall, Farquhar, Finlay, Angus and Patrick.

There are three possible processes which could account for this – migration of Gaels into Inverness, an upward social mobility of Inverness Gaels into positions of influence, or adoption of Gaelic names, and even the Gaelic language, by those of non-Gaelic ancestry. It is likely that all three processes were at work and that the hegemony enjoyed by the English language, if there had ever been such, was breaking down. The respected Inverness historian, the late Evan Barron, estimated that in the 15th Century the burgesses of the town, that is those with special rights in trade and government, formed only about one-fifth of the population. The other four-fifths were "persons of all sorts and conditions, mainly of the poorest class – labourers, fishers, servants, broken men from the clans, and beggars." The evidence points to Gaelic being widely spoken among these people. Indeed, it is likely that it was the majority tongue in this group and, therefore, in the town as a whole.

In the 16th Century, non-Gaelic names such as Marshall, Fleming, Dunbar, Cuthbert, Vass and Winchester, were still dominant within the merchant community, but the Gaels were growing in prominence. John McGillewe enters the Records of the Town Council in 1556; from the records we learn that his father Donald was a burgess as early as 1521, and that he was engaged in a legal struggle with another burgess of Gaelic heritage, Alexander McGillemartin.

Among the burgesses in 1605 were Findlay dhu-Vic Phaill (Black Finlay MacPhail) and Andrew Vic-William-Mor. The latter name is a Gaelic patronymic of the type only found today in the most strongly Gaelic-speaking communities; it means Andrew, son of big William. The "Vic" (here wrongly applied, as it should be "Mac") is actually "Mhic", the genitive form of "Mac" and means "of the son".

There is much evidence of the Gaelic patronymic in 16th Century Inverness. In 1574 one John Dow McRorye (*Iain Dubh mac Ruairidh,* Black John, son of Roddy) was permitted to set up a stall for the sale of merchandise. Five years later he was joined in his trade by Allister McConquhie (*Alasdair mac Dhonnchaidh*; Alexander son of Duncan). Allister's father, just to establish the validity of the patronymic, was known as Duncan McConquhie Dowe ie *Donnchadh mac Dhonnchaidh Dhuibh* (Duncan, son of Black Duncan). There are many more examples of such Gaelic personal nomenclature in the Inverness records.

Further evidence for Gaelic having a significant presence in Inverness lies in the use of the feminine form of surnames, a practice which did not pass into general usage in English. For example, today, while Donald MacLeod would be called *Dòmhnall MacLeòid* in Gaelic, his sister Kate MacLeod would be *Ceit*

"William McPhadrik, William Boy McPhaill, Murreall Neyn Barroun, ar followit for the wrangus tacking of thair malt to the myln of Kilbean ..."

This note from the Burgh Court Books of 4 Dec 1568 is one of many examples which demonstrate the strength of Gaelic personal nomenclature at the time. "Boy" is buidhe (yellow-haired) and the female is Muriel the daughter of Barron. They had wrongly attended the Mill of Bucht, then commonly called the Myln of Kilbean after the Gaelic Muileann Chill Bheathain.

NicLeòid, employing the feminc *Nic* rather than *Mac*. Women must have often been referred to after the Gaelic manner in Inverness in the 16th and 17th centuries, for the records contain references to such as Maggie Nic Gillewe (a daughter of burgess John McGillewe), Agnes Nic Intoishie (Agnes Mackintosh), Catherine Nic Cowll (Catherine MacDougall) and Mòr Nic Loid (Sarah MacLeod).

The same applies to the appearance of the feminine patronymic in the Town Records. Here we see an anglicised form of the Gaelic *nighean* (daughter), as in Katherine nien Donald (Katherine, daughter of Donald), Effie nyn Hendryk Moir (Effie, daughter of Big Henry) and Janet nyn Gillepatrick Crowbach (Janet, daughter of lame Gillepatrick). In 1577, two of the licensed bakers in the town were Agnes Neyn Fynla Moir (Agnes, daughter of big Finlay) and Beak Crowbycht ie *Beathag Chrùbach* (lame Rebecca). Beathag was not even given an English surname – she was simply listed in the nickname form which would be recognised by the people of the town.

William Mackay, who was among the founders of the Gaelic Society of Inverness (as well as being the founder of a prominent legal firm in the town), researched this aspect of the town's history in some detail and was of the opinion that "southern settlers", as he referred to them, married Gaelic-speaking women, producing Gaelicised offspring who were generally given Gaelic names. Thus we read of Finlay Gibson, Ewen Taylor, Finlay Man,

William Mackay, one of Inverness's most prominent Gaels in the late 19th Century.

Manis Blunt, Patrick Skinner, Janet Nyk Craigie and Morreacht nyn Brand.

Naturally enough, many of Inverness's transgressors were Gaels. On 27 February 1563, one John Bane (probably *Iain Bàn*, fair John) gave surety for Donald McConyll McInnes, ie *Dòmhnall mac Dhòmhnaill mhic Aonghais* (Donald, son of Donald, son of Angus) that he would not be found selling goods in, or near, the town. At the same time, one James Paterson did likewise for Gillespyk McConquhie Roy, *Gilleasbuig mac Dhonnchaidh Ruaidh,* (Archibald, son of Red Duncan). On 18 June 1613, Donald McAine McWilliam vic Miben was indicted as a "common vagibond and masterless thief" and sentenced to "have his ear nailed to the pillory and thereafter to be scourged through the four streets of the town and banished", and on 2 October 1615 Allister McConil vic Andrew vic Finlay was found guilty of multiple theft, including a horse from Easter Drakies, and sentenced to be drowned at the bridge.

Not for the last time, poaching was the subject of legal sanction in the 16th century. One John Crom (bent John), was found guilty of stealing salmon from the cruives on the river Ness and sentenced to have his ear nailed to the trone (the market place) and to be left to tear his lug from the nail. And a Dutch mariner visiting the town in 1568, one Christofer Wafer, had cause to dislike certain Inverness Gaels. He was threatened by John Ard (tall John) and Alexander McGilleworrycht and, worse than that, attacked with a sword by Gillecallum McDavid Moyr (Gilliecallum, son of Big David).

It is likely that Gillecallum attended his arraignment in glaslawes – the anglicised form of the Gaelic *glas-làmh* (handcuffs), a word which appears in the Inverness records. Whether or not he was considered a skemlar (*sgimilear*, a parasite) is not recorded; neither is his possible possession of a *cabar* (pole) or a *clag* (bell). These are all Gaelic words which appear in the records, along with *larach* (site or stance), a word still used in Inverness title deeds in the modern era.

But the town records do not form the only concrete evidence of the vigour of Gaelic within Inverness. In 1656 the diglottic situation was noted by Thomas Tucker who wrote that, "Ane halfe of the people understand not one another." The traveller Thomas Kirk, who visited the town in 1677, noted that the numerically dominant tongue was Gaelic. "All in the town of Inverness do generally use that language," he wrote, "except some of the better sort, that can speak Scottish [ie English]."

20

The Witches of the Millburn

The Clachnacuddin Nonagerian, John Maclean, tells us of the witches of Millburn whose deeds and fate are also recorded in oral tradition. They lived in Maclean's grandmother's day which must have been early in the 18th Century. Two sisters, one of whom was known as Creibh Mhòr, dwelt in one of the several "bothies" in the valley of the Mill Burn and practised their art both there and in the adjacent glen through which the "Allt Mournaic/ Aultmuniack" (probably *Allt Muineach*, see p. 46) then flowed. While playing in that burn, some children found a *corp crèadha* (or a *bodachan* as Maclean has it), a clay figurine stuck over with pins which was used in earlier times as a means of placing a curse on a particular victim, which might even cause that person's death. One of the children admitted seeing her grandmother making such an object, word got around, and Creibh Mhòr was arrested and tortured in order to extract a confession of witchcraft.

Creibh resisted but her sister was likewise tortured, and she confessed to the crime, admitting that the effigy represented Cuthbert of Castlehill *(Mac Sheòrsa Chàisteil Stìll)*. According to Maclean, the sister watched Creibh being burned to death at the stake on Barn Hill and cursed both Bailie David Fraser and the Cuthberts before being consumed by the flames. In line with the curse, Fraser, the civic magistrate, sold no more goods from his shop, and George Cuthbert, Sheriff Depute of Inverness-shire, fell from his horse and died at the western end of the glen of the Allt Muineach in 1748.

However, Creibh Mhòr pops up in the oral tradition as having escaped her sentence and fled to Strathnairn. In a Gaelic story related by Donnchadh Mac a' Bheathain of Croachy, she uttered a curse against the landlord and farmer of Flichity (I have here standardised the Gaelic): "Fhad 's a bhios an t-allt aig Flicheadaidh a' ruith dhan taobh tuath, bidh mollachd air Flicheadaidh. Ma gheibh an tuathanach math, chan fhaigh an tighearna, agus ma gheibh an tighearna math, chan fhaigh an tuathanach." (As long as the burn at Flichity runs to the north, a curse will be on Flichity. If the farmer does well, the landlord will not, and if the landlord does well, the farmer will not).

At this time the Anglophone authorities were regularly referring to the Gaelic language as "Irish" and even to the Gaelic-speaking people as "Irish people" or "Irishes". The intellectual distancing of English and Scots-speaking people from Gaelic, which had been the majority tongue in Scotland not too long before, and the speech of its monarchs until the end of the eleventh century, was now proceeding apace, creating a legacy which still resonates across much of the country today.

The first reference to a church in Inverness whose services were entirely in Gaelic occurs in 1639 although it is likely that the language was employed in worship before that year. In 1640 the Provost, James Ross, complained to the Presbytery about the ruinous state of the building which was, in any case, too small to accommodate the "common and Irish people" who wished to attend services. In February 1641 the Presbytery created a post for a Gaelic-speaking minister and enlarged the choir of the High Church to accommodate the congregation. The Rev. Duncan McCulloch was the first to occupy the post but he was transferred to the parish of Urquhart and Glenmoriston in 1647, leaving the Gaels of Inverness without a minister for some considerable time.

The situation of the Rev. Robert Baillie illustrates that the Church on occasions put political considerations before those of language; it also gives us the first possible enumeration of Gaelic-speakers in the town. Baillie was translated from Lanarkshire to take up a ministry to the Gaels of Inverness in 1703, a move which horrified him as he spoke no Gaelic whatsoever. The Church, however, was attempting to sideline the current Gaelic-speaking minister, the Rev. Hector Mackenzie, because of his alleged aversion to the Crown and sympathy for Episcopalianism. The Church authorities had resolved to remove such men and the General Assembly of 1699 had permitted the use of "ministers or probationers, who have somewhat of the Irish language, but not a facility to preach in it".

It appears that Baillie did not even satisfy the first requirement and he wrote to the Church's Commission for the North, saying that his "transportation hath brought fifteen hundred poor Irishes in this place to a deplorable hardship." In a pamphlet called *Information of the Circumstances of Inverness* (1704), he wrote that the population of the entire parish was about 4,840. Of the sector of the population aged fourteen and over, he estimated that there were "3,000 who understand not English" and that they consisted of "1,247 within the town of Inverness and 1,753 in the Countrey." These figures were in addition to a bilingual

> *There are ... about 3,000 who understand not English ... whereof 1,247 within the town of Inverness and 1,753 in the Countrey.*
>
> Rev. Robert Baillie, 1704

congregation of some 900 persons, of whom 800 lived in the town and 100 in the country. He concluded that only forty town-dwellers (aged fourteen and over) were monoglot English-speakers.

It may be that Baillie, who was keen to leave his charge, deliberately overestimated the Gaelic figures, and they should be accompanied by an appropriate health warning; for example, the overall population of the town may have been higher than quoted, although Dr Webster's "survey" of 1754, which gave 9,730, seems to stretch reality, given that it was counted at 9,633 in 1831, and estimated by "actual survey" in 1791 at 5,107, according to the Statistical Account.

According to Baillie, of the 3,940 people of fourteen years and over in his parish "census" (including rural areas), only 1% were entirely ignorant of Gaelic, 23% were bilingual and 76% were monoglot Gaels. In the town itself, of the 2,087 inhabitants of 14 years and over, only 2% spoke no Gaelic, 38% were bilingual and 60% were monoglot Gaelic-speakers.

It is likely that a considerable portion of the bilingual element was made up of those who preferred to use English but who were capable of speaking Gaelic in order that they might engage in discourse with their neighbours. It is also clear, however, that there was a considerable number of people living within the town of Inverness at the turn of the 18th Century who spoke no English whatsoever. This is unlikely to have been an overnight phenomenon and it is reasonable to suggest that, over the long history of the town, there were several thousand inhabitants who lived their entire lives through the Gaelic language, without ever speaking English. Incidentally, Baillie's supplications were ignored and he remained in post. In 1706 the Rev. William Stuart of Kiltearn parish was moved to Inverness to minister to its sizeable Gaelic population and, presumably, to remove their "deplorable hardship".

Of course, there are accounts which seem to conflict with Baillie's picture of the town. A traveller, John Mackay, wrote in 1717 that "they speak as good

English here as at London and with an English accent and ever since Oliver Cromwell was here they are in their manners and dress entirely English". One has to wonder if he failed to mix with the poorer elements of the town, as Captain Edmund Burt, an Englishman who was stationed in Inverness in the 1730s, during the construction of some of the Highlands' military roads, and whose letters to a friend were published in 1754, wrote clearly of a bilingual situation: "… although they speak English, there are scarce any who do not understand the Irish Tongue; and it is necessary that they should do so, to carry on their Dealings with the neighbouring Country People; for within less than a Mile of the Town, there are few who speak any English at all."

Washing clothes in the river in Burt's day. Were these very tubs rested on Clach na Cùdainn?

The bilingualism of some of the town bailies of this period is demonstrated by the tale of an Inverness woman, Anne McKay, in whose cellar two Jacobite soldiers were kept prisoner following the Battle of Culloden. A plot was hatched to free one of them, in which McKay agreed to assist by distracting the sentry. Following the escape, the Skye-born woman, who had lived in Inverness for a considerable time, was brought in front of a military officer for questioning. She, however, was unable to answer as she spoke not a word of English. In order to conduct the interview, the authorities called upon Bailie Fraser to question her in Gaelic.

But, regardless of such bilingualism, Gaels never controlled Inverness politically. On the Town Council of 1660, for example, we have five Cuthberts (called *Mac Sheòrsa* by local Gaels), two Baillies, two Roses and a Lockhart, Hepburn, Fraser, Polson, Robertson, Grant, Cowy and Chapman. Some of these men would have been bilingual, but they would have conducted their business largely in English, except where required to deal with monoglot Gaelic-speakers.

But Gaelic appears to have had the numbers among the common people, and the numerical dominance was likely retained through much, if not all, of the 18th century. In 1798, Thomas Garnett, Professor of Natural Philosophy and Chemistry in the Royal Institution of Great Britain, travelled through the Highlands and wrote of Inverness that, "English and Gaelic are spoken here promiscuously, though the language of the country people is Gaelic." He also noted that "English is spoken with great purity, both with respect to pronunciation and grammar. This may be owing to two causes; in the first place it is not the mother tongue, but is learned by book ... and not from common conversation." It is interesting to note that he gave no credence to the popular, if slightly eccentric, view that it was Cromwell's English soldiers, who had been stationed at the citadel in Inverness for a few years, who had been responsible for the reputedly high standard of the townsfolk's spoken English.

English and Gaelic are spoken here promiscuously, though the language of the country people is Gaelic.

Thomas Garnett 1798

The soldiers were not without impact on Inverness, however. It was they who reputedly introduced an efficient and humane form of animal slaughter which they conducted on a hill near Clachnaharry on the Muirtown estate. This was given the name Knockgur *(Cnoc a' Ghaorra)*, "the hill of the gore". As late as the 19th Century, the Inverness slaughtermen, who were descendants of the original abattoir operators, were still known locally as *Clann Mhic an t-Sasannaich* ("the children of the Englishman's son").

Inverness was also the birthplace and dwelling place of a number of notable Gaelic bards, although sadly little is known about some of them. An example is *am Bàrd Dòmhnallach* ("the MacDonald poet) who lived in the 18th Century. The love song *Thèid mi a dh'Inbhir Nis seachdain o màireach* ("I will go to Inverness tomorrow week") belongs to the same century, although its author remains unidentified. And Invernessian Colin Beaton was among many Gaelic poets who wrote pro-Jacobite verse following the Battle of Culloden, in his case some seven years after that fateful day.

Janet MacDougall *(Seònaid Dhùghallach)* is another who wrote several Gaelic poems praising members of the local gentry, among whom was Maria Baillie, of whom the bardess writes "is binne labhras Beurla 's Gàidhlig", demonstrating that members of this class were still bilingual at the time. Maria died in 1835. Alexander MacOldonich of Aultanulit (probably *Allt an Ionnlaid*, "the washing burn" in Muirtown) was another whose poetry appeared in the 19th Century although he probably wrote it in the century previous to that.

Lachlan MacLachlan was born in about 1729 in Balachlan, at Mile End, Kinmylies. As a teenager he observed Jacobite soldiers being cut down by Hanoverian troops upon their fleeing from the Culloden battlefield. He was a schoolmaster at Culduthel and Abriachan, and he composed a number of sacred poems in which he attacked the notion of patronage and the "moderates" within the Church. One of his grandsons, Rev. Dr Thomas MacLachlan (1816-86), was a leading Gaelic scholar and a Moderator of the Free Church. Another bard with a connection to Abriachan was Thomas MacDonald, known locally after his dwelling place as *Tòmas an Tòdhair.*

Kenneth Mackenzie was an Inverness bard of considerable note; indeed he was the only native of the area to be included in the classic national anthology *Sàr-obair nam Bàrd Gaelach* ("The Beauties of Gaelic Poetry"). He was born at *Caisteal na Lethoir* (now erroneously anglicised as Castle Heather) in 1758, and his poetry gives us an insight into the original pronunciation of some local place names. He clearly identified with the Gaels of the wider rural Highlands, as evidenced by his powerful work *Òran do na Caoraich Mhòra* in which he berated the landlords' policy of clearing the people to replace them by sheep. In the

MAIREARAD MHOLACH MHIN.

LUINNEAG.

Mo rùn Mairearad mhìn mholach,
'S mo rùn Mairearad mholach mhìn,
Mo rùn Mairearad mhìn mholach,
'S iomadh fear a th'air a tì.

'S ioma gille tapaidh bàrra-ghast,
Eadar Dealganros nam frìth,
S ceann Loch-nis nam bradan tarra-gheal,
Tha le ime-cheist air a tì.
  Mo rùu, etc.

'S àile chumainn trod ri naoinear,
Ged' a dh'aomadh iad gu strì,
'S cha leag mì gu bràth le duin' i,
On a dh'fhàs i molach mìn.
  Mo rùn, etc.

'S truagh nach sinn bha air àiridh,
Air ar fàgail ann leinn fhìn,
S chumadh ì bho'n fhuachd mi sàbhailt,
On a dh'fhàs i molach mìn.
  Mo rùn, etc.

Ge d' a gheibhinn tàirgse bhàintigh'rn,
'S neo-ar-thaing a bheirinn d'i, [drais,
'S mòr gum b'fhearr leam Nic-'Ill-Eann-
Tha na th'ann d'i molach mìn.
  Mo rùn, etc.

Buaidhean mo chruinneig cha léir dhomh,
An cuir an géill cha dean mi 'n inns',
Thug nàdur dh'i tuigs as reasan,
Agus ceill nam beusan fìllt.
  Mo rùn, etc.

Tha i sgeudaichte le h-àilteachd,
'S a càirdeas mar ghràn air pill,
Séimh, fallain, ùr, 's cumaite dh'fhàs i,
O mullach gu sàil a buinn.
  Mo rùn, etc.

Part of a ditty written by Kenneth Mackenzie, the only Inverness bard to feature in the classic 19th Century anthology of Gaelic bàrdachd "The Beauties of Gaelic Poetry", edited by John Mackenzie of Gairloch. Poetry is one source of information on local place names: the author mentions two places in this poem - Dealganros (the original Gaelic for Dalcross) on the sixth line and Cuilodair (Culloden), later in the poem (not included here). Mackenzie was much influenced by the poetry of Alasdair Mac Mhaighstir Alasdair and Duncan Bàn MacIntyre. He spent years at sea, before entering the army and later becoming a postmaster in Ireland.

words *chaidh Gàidhlig às an fhasan aig buidhinn nan ad 's nan cleòc* ("Gaelic went out of fashion among the people of the hats and cloaks"), he commented on a social change that was having serious cultural repercussions across the entire Gaidhealtachd.

Colonel James Fraser of Culduthel, an acquaintance of Mackenzie, was obviously exempt from the criticism, for he composed Gaelic verse (as had his father, Captain Alexander Fraser, before him), and he himself was the subject of a song – *Òran do Chornailfhear Seumas Friosal, Chuldaothal* by a Lachlan MacShuine (who cannot be identified), which was included in a collection of Gaelic songs published in Inverness in 1806. Incidentally, this song gives us a clear indication of the pronunciation of the original Gaelic name for Culduthel.

William Mackenzie, the "Leys Bard", who was famous for his spiritual poems, was born at Baile Mhic Phàdraig at Balloan in 1748. He was the schoolmaster at Leys for forty years and died in Inverness in 1838. A well close to the private road leading into Leys Castle was known as *Fuaran a' Mhaighstir* (the Schoolmaster's Well), and was reputedly named after Mackenzie. While much of his verse survives, the same cannot be said for *Iain Bàn Friseal* (John Fraser), tenant farmer of Balphadrig in the Kinmylies district, or of another John Fraser who had a croft on the Leachkin. The latter died in 1871, but Gaelic was then still strong enough in the area for his son to be known (after the father) by the nickname *Seoc a' Phunndair* (Jock of the Pounder, ie a shepherd or cattleherd who is employed to confine straying livestock).

Incidentally, the existence of recorded characters whose only known appellation was a Gaelic nickname is another strand of evidence for the strength of the language in the town of Inverness. One of the most famous is Finlay Dhu (*Fionnladh Dubh*, black Finlay) who was responsible in 1665 for the "rude ryot and slaughter at a fair in Inverness called the Cabog Day", according to the Wardlaw Manuscript. Finlay picked up a big round cheese (*càbag* in Gaelic) at a bread and cheese stall in the Horse Market to the south of the Castle and "whether designedly or by negligence" let it fall from his grip and run down the hill into the river. The woman stall-keeper demanded payment, which Finlay refused, and the ensuing argument ended up in a riot in which the town guards killed two men.

Other characters in the town's history are remembered today by their Gaelic nicknames. *Teàrlach Sùileach* (sharp-sighted Charles) looked after the Provost's cattle, *Seun nam Pòcaidean* (Jenny of the pockets) had outer garments which were eccentrically covered in pockets from her neck to her ankles, and *Alasdair Beag* (Little Sandy) of the Haugh used a room in the castle at night as a workshop in which he, by his own account, regularly met the silent ghost of a dead officer. In the case of *Iain Bàn an t-Iasgair* (fair John the fisherman), a salmon fisher on the Ness, we happen to know his "official" name – John Paterson. His son, James, born in Muirtown early in the 19th Century, enjoyed a reputation of sorts for writing verse in English.

Gaelic nicknames were still being created in the town of Inverness in the middle of the 19th Century. An example is the *Taillear Tàstain* (the "shilling tailor") whose official name was Murdo Graham. As his nickname suggests, he rarely charged more than a shilling. He was recalled by John Fraser whose book *Reminiscences of Inverness*, published in 1905 and relating "a walk through Inverness sixty years ago", affords a fascinating picture of the town around the time that John Maclean was recording his own memories of earlier times in his *Reminiscences of a Clachnacuddin Nonagenarian*. Indeed, Fraser and Maclean engage in "conversation" in Fraser's book and, together, these two publications provide important evidence relating to the social and linguistic history of Inverness through the 18th and early 19th centuries. Fraser gives us accounts of others with Gaelic nicknames, such as *Thomas Tigh-chinn*, a Thomas Fraser, weaver, who lived at the head of a close on Tomnahurich Street, *Ali Beag na Creag* (Little Sandy of the Crag) of Dunain and *William Ruadh* (William MacDonald), a cobbler in Young Street. There was William Ross, better known as the *Brocair* (the badger or fox-hunter), Dr. Roderick Fraser or *Rory Bruich* and *Bean a' Mhuilleir* (the miller's wife), a Mrs Maclean whose duty was to patrol the Little Green near Ness Walk at night to ensure that none of the community's laundry went missing.

Fraser is also one of the few writers to record some actual Gaelic speech of the period. He recalls meeting with Angus Calder, flesher, of Castle Street, in his "killing shed" on King Street, when Angus sent a lad to the shop to buy a paper for him. The boy, ironically known as *Iain Sgoilear* (John Scholar) as he had learning difficulties, was brandishing a wooden board on which the letters of the alphabet were written. Fraser considered he had no great "prospect of ever getting as far as X,Y, Z without a blunder, although his mother, whose only language is the vernacular, often says, 'Tha Iain a' fàs na sgoilear math le a leabhar-maide' (John is getting a good scholar with his wooden book)."

However, a comment of Fraser's gives an indication of the linguistic change occurring in Inverness, with many of the younger generation being unable to speak Gaelic. He gives an account of a small shop on King Street belonging to "Marsali Ruadh (or 'Red May' as the young people call her)."

An account by the Rev. James Hall published in 1807 suggests there may have been less of the bilingualism associated with the town a century before. "At Inverness," he wrote, "I found a strange medley of the Scotch and English language spoken in the streets…there are, as it were, two towns, and two different people, as the people that come from the country, and intend to speak Gaelic, live in one end of the town, and those that cannot, or do not intend to speak it, live in the other". The terminology had by now changed once more, so that Gaelic was no longer "Irish" but "Scotch".

Despite the weakening linguistic situation, Inverness in the mid to late 19th Century still bore intimate connections to some of Gaeldom's most celebrated figures. Among them was *Màiri Mhòr nan Òran*, Mary MacPherson the Skye poetess, who spent a quarter of a century living in the town married to Isaac MacPherson, shoemaker, before his death. Several of her songs relate to Inverness, and most particularly to the political battles involving land law reform candidates, such as the Gaelic-speaking Charles Fraser-Mackintosh of Drummond, whose cause she championed.

Màiri Mhòr's headstone in the Chapel Yard cemetery

Drawing upon the historic reputation of *Clach na Cùdainn*, the stone now situated on a pedestal outside the Town Hall, as the town's palladium, she referred in her poetry to the people of Inverness as *clann na "Cloiche"*, the children of the "Stone". Now one of the famous stones of the town, visited over the years by many Scots who cherish Mary's legacy, is the headstone adorning her own grave in Chapel Yard which was placed there by Charles Fraser-Mackintosh in tribute to her following her death in 1898.

Inverness also boasts a rich thread of Gaelic stories, of which a few have survived. Many of them centred traditionally around Tomnahurich, a striking glacial esker to the west of the Ness which became identified by the Gaels as a *sìthean* (fairy hill). It had a nationwide reputation as an abode of the fairies and was reckoned by local people to be the last resting place of Fionn MacCumhail and his heroic companions. Stories based around the hill, and which are still told today in both languages, include *Na Fìdhlearan agus Sìthichean Thom na h-Iùbhraich* (the Fiddlers and the Fairies of Tomnahurich), *Gort a' Bhainne* (the Milk Famine) and *Aonghas Mòr agus na Sìthichean* (Big Angus and the Fairies).

Other localities in Inverness also had fairy associations. An example was an ancient barn behind the West Church known as *An Subhal Daraich* (the oak barn), which was reputed to have been constructed in a single night by the Tomnahurich fairies and which was a prohibited location after nightfall. However it might have been constructed, it was owned in the mid-18th Century by a Duncan Robertson who was the first man to make a horse-drawn carriage available for hire in the town. The local name for his vehicle is not recorded, but a private gig owned by the laird at Muirtown was known in Inverness as *an Sgùlan Dubh* ("the black basket").

In addition to tales of fairies, Gaelic tradition also attested to the death of the last wolf in Scotland occurring in the parish of Inverness, not far from Kinmylies but, as this claim is also made for at least a dozen other localities in the Highlands, one should perhaps not make too much of it!

Other stories existed within local tradition and, in keeping with the fairy legends, they often involved hardship affecting the populace. One such was the account of an unfortunate who was locked in the miserable dungeon which had been constructed between the second and third arches of the seven-arched stone bridge built across the Ness in 1685 (and later destroyed by a flood). He met his fate in about 1715 (for which particular crime is unknown) and he could be heard by the townsfolk in winter as he cried out the sad refrain *"casan fuara, casan fuara"* (cold

Tomnahurich and the Fairies

Tomnahurich had a national reputation as a place associated with the supernatural, and it is still considered to be a "fairy hill" by many Invernessians. The best known of the surviving traditional stories is *Na Fìdhlearan agus Sìthichean Thom na h-Iùbhraich* (The Fiddlers and the Fairies of Tomnahurich), which concerns two fiddlers from Glen Feshie in Badenoch who are driven by poverty to busk on the streets of Inverness. At day's end they meet a fairy man on the Ness bridge and he convinces them to follow him to a place where fiddlers are in demand and where they will make money. They are led into the bowels of Tomnahurich where they play all night in a hall of gold and crystal to the fairy dancers. As day breaks, the fiddlers are asked hurriedly to leave, and each is given a bag of gold.

However, when they go home they see the graves of their wives and children in the cemetery, for a hundred years have passed in the real world for the one night in the fairy realm, and they themselves are destroyed when the minister, whose sermon they are listening to, utters the word "God".

Another story located in the same vicinity is *Gort a' Bhainne* (The Milk Famine) in which a farmer produces much more milk than any other in the area, it is said, because his grass is under a magic spell. Suddenly the cows stop producing, the milk dries up all over Inverness, and a year goes past without a child getting any to drink. The fairies are blamed.

One summer afternoon, the once-productive farmer sees a small man walking past him with a hawthorn branch over his shoulder which seems to have a weight attached to it, although nothing is visible. The farmer whips out a knife, cuts the end of the branch off, and the wee man keeps on walking until he goes out of sight on the Leachkin. But the piece of branch at the farmer's feet suddenly starts gushing milk which runs all the way into the Ness. The cattle start producing once more, and the milk famine is over.

A third story is *Aonghas Mòr agus Na Sìthichean* (Big Angus and the Fairies). This concerns a struggle between Angus, a shepherd near Tomnahurich, and the fairies, who threaten to take away his wife and child. Angus eventually throws off the spell by hearing the Fairy Queen sing her secret song at *Drochaid an Easain Duibh* (the bridge of the small dark waterfall) and telling her that her magic is now known to him.

feet, cold feet). He would have undoubtedly benefitted from some items of footwear which in Inverness were commonly known by their Gaelic names. The Clachnacuddin nonagenarian, John Maclean, tells us that the cheap leather brogues were called *bròagan dubha* (black shoes) whereas the more expensive soled variety, which might cost up to 2s 9d per pair, were *brogain Sasgunnach* (i.e. *bròagan Sasannach,* English shoes).

Maclean's reminiscences include a story from the 18th Century in which a pair of the "English shoes" were acquired in a most macabre manner. An Irishman called Shearfield, who had been in the Hanoverian army, murdered his wife in the town and was hanged at the gibbet, where his corpse was left to dangle. A Highlander ("from a neighbouring parish") was unable to pull the expensive footwear from the corpse, and he cut the feet off at the ankles in order to fulfil his desire for the *bròagan.*

Some of the many transgressors who were despatched at the very same gibbet are best remembered by their Gaelic appellations – *Mac Iain Ruaidh,* the Black Isle freebooter, and the outlaw *Archie Bui* being two of the most notorious. The site of the gibbet, called Barnhill in English, was known in Gaelic as *Tom nan Ceann,* the hill of the heads, from the original form of execution, which was beheading.

One of the most severe of the sheriffs, who would often recommend a short sojourn at the gibbet for convicted criminals was a Mackenzie of Kilcoy known as the *Shirra Dhu (Siorra' Dubh)* – the "black sheriff", the colour being a commentary on his character, rather than the shade of his hair. He, however, met his match in a certain Samuel Cameron whom he had condemned to death in Inverness, but who had escaped to roam the wild hills around Abriachan. Cameron ambushed the sheriff on Loch Ness-side and made him promise to publicly declare the outlaw a free man at the market cross in Inverness on the following Friday, a demand to which the sheriff acquiesced.

Another prisoner, who is remembered by the Gaelic sobriquet *Dòmhnall Sgoilear,* was at one time confined in the dungeon below the bridge over the Ness, where local boys would tease him by dangling pieces of bread in front of the bars of his cage. When later in the town jail, he came to a tragic end while attempting to free himself on the night before his execution. A rope by which he was lowering himself from his place of confinement proved to be too short and *Dòmhnall* fell to his death on the street below.

The early 19th Century was a time of great change. The linguistic shift from Gaelic to English was replicated widely across the town at this time. In 1828, a *Short Account of the Town of Inverness,* published in Edinburgh, said that the language "generally used by the common people is the Gaelic, but the English language is spoken by the superior classes, with a purity of pronunciation not to be equalled in any part of Scotland. The Gaelic is also spoken here in its utmost purity - both languages are so familiar, that it is common to hear children at play, put a question in Gaelic, and receive an answer in English." According to the *New Statistical Account* of 1835, in the "remoter parts of the parish, and by some of the poorer classes in town, the Gaelic language is exclusively spoken, but is fast wearing out, and by the rising generation English is almost universally preferred, especially in the town of Inverness, where many of them are wholly ignorant of Gaelic."

> *Gaelic is also spoken here in its utmost purity - both languages are so familiar, that it is common to hear children at play, put a question in Gaelic, and receive an answer in English.*
>
> *Inverness 1828*

But Gaelic was still a significant part of life in Inverness in the 19th Century, despite a growing body of those who could not speak it. There is an amusing tale of how a trombone player from the town, one Jockie Cumming, not himself a Gaelic-speaker, wrote a Strathspey tune called "Cutty Sark" after hearing a quarrel in Gaelic between two women who lived in the Meal Market Close off the High Street – a Nannie Kennedy and Mary Fraser or "Mary Cod". One of Jockie's sons later wrote that his father was "so tickled with the scene and sounds that immediately on getting to his home a few doors further down the same thoroughfare, he noted down a musical imitation of the strange scene he had seen, and the Gaelic expletives he had listened to, and *Cutty Sark* was the result."

Gaelic also had an important place in the religious life of Inverness. The town's Gaelic congregation was so large that it could often not be accommodated in the Gaelic Church (now a book shop at the northern end of Church Street).

34

The old Gaelic Church in Church Street

This is despite the fact that this building could seat some 1,220 persons. Through much of the 19th Century there are records of large religious congregations of Gaels in outdoor locations such as the yard of the High Church, the Chapel Yard, now a cemetery, and in the grounds of Bell's School, now the Town Library.

John Maclean, who was born in 1746, describes in his *Reminiscences of a Clachnacuddin Nonagenarian* how in his "youthful days two Gaelic congregations at one time assembled in separate parts of the Chapel Yard, listening to the discourses, preparatory to the celebration of the Lord's Supper." He also relates the existence of a vault in the south side of the Gaelic church in which an oak coffin called *a' Chiste Chumant'* (the common coffin) was stored; from this simple box, the bodies of the poor, or strangers to the town, were slipped into a grave. He also tells of how the bodies of drowned persons were deposited in the Gaelic Church before being claimed, and of how a minister who was endowed with the *dà-shealladh* (second sight) foretold a fisherman's death.

The Clachnacuddin Nonagenarian

Much fascinating information relating to Inverness place names, and to the history and heritage of the city, is to be found in a slim publication, first produced in 1842 and entitled *Reminiscences of a Clachnacuddin Nonagenarian*. The elderly gentleman in question is John Maclean who was 96 when his memories of Inverness and its surrounds were put into print. It is not insignificant that he, or Mr Bond of the *Inverness Herald*, who ghost-scripted the volume, chose to associate him with Clachnacuddin, or *Clach na Cùdainn* (see pages 4 and 66), as this ancient stone was for long considered the most unique and powerful symbol of Inverness.

Although written in English, Maclean's account is peppered with Gaelic names of people, places and events. A brief reference to his own life history is given in the form of a conversation between himself and John Fraser, in the latter's 1905 publication *Reminiscences of Inverness*, another book with much to interest the student of social history which looks back to the town as it was in the 1840s.

"I was born in the parish of Wardlaw, or Kirkhill, on January 7th, 1746, just about three months before that ever-memorable battle [Culloden]," Maclean tells Fraser. "I was brought up a great deal with my grandfather, who was born a few years previous to the Revolution of 1688." From his grandfather's stories, in addition to his own great lifespan, his "memory" of local characters and events stretched back into the 17th Century.

Maclean became a tailor and went into Inverness a lot on business, before eventually settling in the town. He could remember when there were only four inhabited houses on the west side of the river, he could recall criminals being confined in the dungeon below the bridge over the river and he claimed to have reached sixty years of age before the first coach started to run between Inverness and Perth. He could also recall the first appearance of an umbrella in the Highland capital! The Clachnacuddin Nonagenarian lived to be a centenarian and in his final years was often to be seen walking by the river. He died on his 106th birthday and was interred in Greyfriars' Burying Ground.

The Rev. Mr. Morrison of Petty, six miles from Inverness, had unsuccessfully attempted to get the fisherman to "attend the ordinances of the gospel", and one day he told an elder that the man was "at this moment drowned at the new pier of Inverness, and his body will be taken to the Gaelic Church and remain there during the night." The minister was only slightly mistaken; the fisherman's relations in Petty, having heard about his sorry tale, and little doubting the clergyman's abilities, made for Inverness and claimed the body that very evening.

Another character associated with the churches of Inverness, whose real name remains unrecorded, was *Ministear na Feusaig* ("the bearded minister"), an inoffensive and hirsute mendicant of the mid-18th Century who for two years, and in all weathers, retired every evening to sleep in the old High Church, as that building had at that time fallen into disrepair. He was a religious man who often preached during the day in various parts of the town and neighbourhood, and who found no difficulty in obtaining food from local people. The real minister, the Rev. Robert Rose, gave him a set of new clothing at one stage but nothing would convince him to give up his chosen life – that is, until some major restoration work took place on the old High Church, at which point he left Inverness, never to be heard of again.

Despite the fact that Gaelic had for long a central place in religious practice in Inverness, as throughout the Highlands, the church authorities proved themselves at times to be ambivalent about the language. In 1861 the Free Church Presbytery declared their misgivings about the spiritual state of the estimated four thousand people living to the west of the River Ness, which was composed "in a great proportion of the poorer labouring classes." They determined upon holding services in both languages but their attitude to Gaelic was entirely utilitarian. "The use of the former," they wrote of the language, "is found to be indispensable in dealing with the lower classes of this population but it is intended to make English the preferred and predominant language of the mission."

The use of [Gaelic] is found to be indispensable in dealing with the lower classes ... but it is intended to make English the preferred and predominant language of the mission.

Free Church, Inverness, 1861

Prior to the Education (Scotland) Act of 1872, which made no provision for Gaelic in education, and which is seen today as being one of the most damaging acts committed by the national authorities against the language, there was a not insignificant amount of Gaelic taught in schools; much of it was employed to inculcate Christian values among those fortunate enough to receive an education. The Inverness Society for the Support of Gaelic Schools was set up in 1818 with a view to supporting these institutions which were referred to in the vernacular as *Sgoilean Chrìosd* (Schools of Christ).

The main texts used were the Bible, a collection of scripture extracts and the *First Book for Children in the Gaelic Language*, and the schools' objectives and methods were considerably different from what is understood by Gaelic Education today. "Where the English language is sufficiently understood by scholars at entry", it advised, "they shall be first to taught to read the English. But in every other case it shall be required that they be taught to read Gaelic in the first place, thereafter to learn English, Writing and Arithmetic." However, the society ran into financial difficulties within a decade of its establishment, and its functions were eventually absorbed into the work of the Education Committee of the Church of Scotland's General Assembly.

A Gaelic school existed in Clachnaharry as late as 1870, at which stage the village, then just outside the town boundaries, was still recognised as a distinctly Gaelic community ("Gaelic being chiefly spoken here", according to the name books of the Ordnance Survey). The building was the property of Miss Duff of Muirtown House and the subjects taught therein were Gaelic, English Grammar, Arithmetic and Writing. Its average attendance was about 70, all boys.

But the bulk of 18th and 19th Century education was aimed at producing fluency in English. Raining's School, situated at the top of the stairs still named after the exiled Scottish benefactor John Raining whose bequest funded the institution, specifically targetted promising Gaelic-speaking children with a view to turning them into English teachers who might better spread that language across the Highlands. Children from strongly Gaelic-speaking parts of the rural Highlands were deemed to benefit from living in Inverness, as they would be forced to speak English and thereby "get it well rooted." The school was established in 1727 with some eighty pupils.

Despite its lack of legal status, Gaelic was often employed (invariably of necessity) to interview witnesses in court, whether they be from the town or other parts of the Highlands. Of the 76 who testified at the murder trial of Hugh MacLeod of Assynt in 1831, for example, no more than half a dozen did so in English. The hanging of the accused, following a guilty verdict, at the gibbet on the Longman (to which site it had been relocated), was witnessed by between seven and eight thousand people, equivalent to four-fifths of Inverness's population. Before going to the noose, MacLeod addressed the crowd for quarter of an hour in Gaelic. He must have been confident that most, or at least many, could understand his ante-mortem advice to avoid whisky, women, Sabbath-breaking and playing cards.

Even much later in the century, Gaelic was still being used in the courts and, on at least one occasion, no interpreter was called for, as was reported in the Aberdeen Free Press of September 3rd, 1882: "...a case was tried before the Police Court of Inverness on Saturday, when the vulgar tongue was entirely set aside, and the proceedings were conducted in the classic language of Ossian. The case was a trifling one. A sprightly damsel of twenty summers or so, was charged with assaulting a girl with an umbrella, and also kicking her. A material witness refused to give evidence in English, and the Dean of Guild, who heard the case, and who loves the Gaelic, said he would conduct the case in his native tongue. The Superintendent of Police (who prosecuted) asked his questions in Gaelic; the "lady" at the bar was no less glib in her use of the mountain tongue, and the venerable assessor revived his acquaintance with the speech of his boyhood by directing her in that language to avoid making speeches at that stage, but to answer questions. In this way, judge, assessor, fiscal, accused and witness took their part of the case without the aid of an interpreter."

In 1882 the locally-published Celtic Magazine was complaining about the instructions given to census enumerators in the previous year regarding their assessment of whether or not somebody was a Gaelic speaker. "Even in the town of Inverness," the publication claimed, "we personally know of cases where whole families - some numbering nine persons - scarcely any member of whom can express the commonest idea intelligently in English - who are in every sense Gaelic-speaking people only - were returned by the enumerators as English-speaking, while they never utter a word of English unless they are obliged to do so to make themselves understood."

Another group lobbying widely on the census issue was *Comunn Gàidhlig Inbhir Nis* (The Gaelic Society of Inverness), one of the oldest bodies in the Gaelic

Charles Fraser-Mackintosh, Gaelic-speaker and Member of Parliament. As well as having interests in the development of Inverness's urban landscape, he was a member of the Highland Land Law Reform Association, a defender of the rights of rural Gaels, and a member of the Napier Commission whose findings led to the development of crofting legislation.

world, which is still going strongly today. The society was set up in the autumn of 1871 to promote the use of the language and to encourage scholarship within the Gaelic world. While it lobbied on behalf of the Gaelic-speaking poor, its membership was drawn largely from the professional classes of both the town and the wider Highlands.

In 1878, the Society organised what it called "The Great Celtic Demonstration", a large public meeting in the Town House in which resolutions were carried, supporting the promotion of Gaelic in education. The address was given by Charles Fraser-Mackintosh who said that "in Inverness Gaelic is still the spoken language of a large number of its inhabitants; the loved and cherished tongue in which they hold intercourse with each other and, above all, in which they praise and worship God." But the language was never to make the progress in education that it might have, although it is interesting to note that the Gaelic Society in the 1880s was holding its classes for learners in Raining's School, an establishment which had for long aimed to spread the English tongue through the Highlands. This was no doubt due to the fact that the great Celtic scholar, Alexander Macbain, was the school's rector at that time. Macbain, a native of Badenoch, made Inverness his home and while domiciled in the town made a significant contribution to scholarship on place names and philology. His "Etymological Dictionary of the Gaelic Language" remains in demand today and is now available on the internet.

Because the census question of 1881 (the first time it had been posed) referred to "habitual" use of Gaelic, a concept that was widely misunderstood, the figures underestimated the language's strength. Despite this, 29% of the population of Inverness Enumeration District was recorded as Gaelic-speaking. In the centre of the town, in an area bounded by High Street, Baron Taylor's Street, Inglis Street and Church Street, the language was weaker than the average, with some 26.9% "habitually" speaking Gaelic. Only 16% of these Gaels were born in the town. But there were pockets of relative strength. In part of the relatively poor area of Merkinch west of the Ness, the figure for Gaelic-speakers

Dr. Alexander Macbain (1855-1907) - scholar, schoolmaster and author of the Etymological Dictionary of the Gaelic Language

reached 41%, of whom a third were born in Inverness. The local dialect was still well represented but it is clear that it was immigration from the wider Gàidhealtachd that was keeping the language vigorous in the town.

In 1891, with "habitual" removed from the question, Gaelic-speakers comprised 6,356 people within a population of 20,855, some 30.5%. The figure has consistently declined since that time, although it is interesting to note that in the 2001 census 3,593 people in Inverness were recorded as "aged 3 and over and who understand, speak, read or write Gaelic". In the much expanded city of the 21st Century this represents only 8.2% of the populace but, in keeping with the history of Inverness, this is a much higher percentage than exists in any other Scottish city.

By the end of the 19th Century, the "ethnic" Gaelic element was patently in the majority in Inverness. In a survey of the names in the Burgh directory in 1895, Alexander Macbain found that over seventy percent of the inhabitants carried Highland surnames - and that was excluding such names as Morrison, Smith and Anderson which might well have represented Gaelic-speakers. But ancestry had ceased to be a guarantee of linguistic competence. By this stage in the town's history, one could no longer assume that a person with a Highland surname brought up in Inverness could speak the Highland language.

Gaelic did not suddenly die in the 20th Century; indeed, it is still with us today. Through that century and in the early 21st Century, Inverness became established as a national centre for the language. The headquarters of An Comunn Gaidhealach, Comunn na Gàidhlig, Comhairle nan Sgoiltean Àraich, Clì Gàidhlig and Bòrd na Gàidhlig were all established there, emphasising the town's position as the Highland capital. One of Scotland's first Gaelic-medium primary school units was established in Inverness at Central School, and the locally based Highland Council and its predecessor, Highland Regional Council, despite the existence of anti-Gaelic prejudice within their ranks of councillors and officials, have been among the most progressive of Scotland's local authorities with regard to the language.

The number of Gaelic-speakers in the town over the last hundred years has been continually boosted by inward migration of Gaels from other places, and latterly by the advent of Gaelic-medium education, but the widespread community use of the language, and particularly of the local dialect, which lingered on well into the twentieth century in places like Clachnaharry and Merkinch, withered away, a victim of both a prejudiced education system and of social forces which were to strike a severe blow to the language across the length and breadth of the Gàidhealtachd.

That, then, is the historical context upon which we can attempt to understand Inverness's place-name heritage. There is surely enough evidence to lay Macaulay's analysis of Inverness as a "Saxon colony among the Celts", made in the early 19th Century, to rest. He may have moved briefly among some of the "better classes" who spoke laudable English and considered themselves a cut above their Gaelic-speaking peers, but it seems that the linguistic realities of life in Inverness, particularly among the poor who formed the bulk of the population, passed him by. And, indeed, the long history of Gaelic in the town evidently escaped his attention.

It is now time to consider the place names of Inverness, not those officially chosen by the town fathers which were almost universally English, but those which arose by organic processes within the wider community. It is no accident that the majority of them are of Gaelic origin. Indeed, given the language's situation in the town and its surrounds over hundreds of years, we should hardly be surprised that it is so.

Giving children two languages

Mrs Doda Dennis with Class 1 at the Gaelic Medium Unit, Central Primary School. She tells her story below....

"I went to school with not a word of English but I soon learned the language and that gives me an insight into the present-day situation where many pupils come into Gaelic Medium education with no Gaelic. The children go to the nursery here first and then they come to me in Primary 1. They can understand what I am saying and it is my job to encourage them to talk to me. It's marvellous how these children learn a second language at the age of five, and I am convinced that the only way to do it is total immersion. They do not hear a word of English from me and by Christmas they are starting to answer me and talk to me spontaneously in Gaelic. And they progress through the school so that at the end of the seven years they are able to speak, read and write Gaelic. Unfortunately they get very little of the language in secondary education and that remains a cause for concern.

As regards English, we don't teach it until Primary 4 because we believe that the children have to have a strong foundation in the one language first. But we have already taught them the skills of reading and writing in Gaelic and they transfer those skills to English – no bother! And they speak English anyway because it is so strong in the environment outside the school.

This year we have seen two former pupils coming back as teachers. Their Gaelic is fluent and they are excellent teachers – that is surely a mark of success. As to the future, I think Gaelic education will thrive in Inverness, particularly when we get our new Gaelic Medium Primary School, but on one condition – that the Scottish Executive ensures that we have enough teachers with the appropriate language skills and qualifications."

Professor W. J. Watson

Doyen of Scottish Place Name Scholars

William J. Watson *(Uilleam MacBhàtair)* was a Celtic scholar with close connections to Inverness whose reputation was monumental. Much of what we know about the place names of the city and its environs is directly due to his scholarship, and it was while living in Inverness that he laid the foundation of his future reputation. A native Gaelic-speaker, he was born in Easter Ross in 1865 and educated locally before attending the Grammar School of Old Aberdeen.

He graduated in 1886 with First Class Honours from Aberdeen University before going on, with the aid of a scholarship, to further academic attainment at Oxford in the fields of classics and literature. But while at Oxford he attended classes by the great Welsh Celtic scholar, Sir John Rhys, and found himself irrecovably drawn towards studies of the Celts and their heritage.

Between 1894 and 1909 he was Rector of Inverness Royal Academy, during which time he researched place names in the local area, including his home county, leading to the publication of *Place Names of Ross and Cromarty*, which remains in print today. At this time he developed strong associations with the Gaelic Society of Inverness, and always declared himself to be indebted to the scholarship of one of its members, Dr Alexander Macbain, author of the *Etymological Dictionary of the Gaelic Language*.

In 1909 Watson took up the rectorship of Edinburgh Royal High School, and in 1914 he was appointed to succeed the late Donald Mackinnon as Professor of Celtic Languages, Literature and Antiquities in the University of Edinburgh, at that time the only such post in Scotland. From 1916 onwards his research took him towards the eventual publication, in 1926, of *The History of the Celtic Place Names of Scotland*, his greatest work, which is still in demand today.

Watson's second wife was Ella Carmichael, editor of the Celtic Review and daughter of Alexander Carmichael of *Carmina Gadelica* fame. Their son James Carmichael Watson succeeded his father as Professor of Celtic in Edinburgh in 1938 but was killed while serving in the Royal Navy in 1942.

William J. Watson died at his home in Edinburgh in March 1948 and was buried, not in the national capital, but in the Highland capital, on a site of great significance to Gaels – the summit of Tomnahurich. According to his obituary in the Inverness Courier, "… until the end of his days, Professor Watson retained a deep affection for Inverness, and spoke of it always as if it was his spiritual home."

44

Some Place Names No Longer in General Use

There are many Gaelic place names in and around Inverness which have little or no currency today, although they are attested to in maps and documents relating to the history of the area. They give us a picture of the existence of an even more Gaelic landscape in previous centuries than is generally recognised today, and they form an interesting strand of the city's cultural heritage. Where features can be located exactly (and where they still exist), the grid reference is included to allow readers to find them for themselves.

Aldnacreich *Allt na Crìche* Burn of the boundary. With *Allt na h-Imire* (**Auldinhemmerie**) which it joins at 704462, it formed the north-east boundary of the town lands in the 16th century. Flows through Westhill.

Allt na banaraich *Allt na Banaraich* Burn of the milkmaid. Tributary of the Mill Burn which joins that stream at *679437*.

Allt na caillich *Allt na Caillich* Burn of the old woman. The stream which flows through the western portion of Balvonie wood. *697427*

Allt Shiamaidh *Allt Shiamaidh* The meaning of *siamaidh* is obscure. The tributary of the Mill Burn which joins that stream at *686434*.

Inverness panorama ca. 1774, with the Old High Church at left and the ruins of the Castle at right

Auldinhemmerie/Althemrie *Allt na h-Imire* Burn of the ridge or field. One of the old boundary markers of the town lands. Flows into sea at *708472*. Now known in English as the "Cairnlaw Burn".

Aultmurnoche/Altmuniack Probably *Allt Muineach,* thorny burn. This is the stream, now piped underground, which flowed through the dell at Culcabock along which the Perth Road (B9006) passes from the Culcabock roundabout to the Millburn roundabout (at 682458). Other suggestions are the unlikely *Allt Muirneach* (the beloved burn) and *Allt Muranach* (the burn of the sea-bents or marram grass). The latter is a possibility as the seashore of the Moray Firth was once much closer than it is today. This dell and the neighbouring glen of the Mill Burn were long regarded as a stronghold of witchcraft (see p. 21). The thoroughfare where the Fluke Inn (682446) stands on Culcabock Road was called "Fluke Street", reputedly because it led to the ford across this burn. Fluke is thought to be derived from the Gaelic *fliuch* (wet).

Baile Mhic Phadruig *Baile Mhic Phàdraig* Peter/Patrick's son's steading/ township, although Mac Phàdraig may well represent a surname rather than a patronymic. A settlement adjacent to Balloan on the estate of Culduthel. Birthplace of the noted Gaelic bard and teacher, William Mackenzie (The Leys Bard), in 1748.

Balloch, The *Am Bealach* The pass. This is the old name for the pass leading from Castle Street into View Place. The hill at the top of Castle Street was called The Balloch Hill ("Le Ballocis Hill", 1376). *666449*

Bal-na-boddich *Baile nam Bodach* Township of the old men, or possibly of the tenantry. Once part of the farm of Charleston, Kinmylies, as was Ach-na-boddich (*Achadh nam Bodach,* field of the old men/tenantry).

Balnahairn Meaning uncertain but possibly *Baile na h-Àirne,* Township of the sloe or blackthorn (*Prunus spinosa*). Close to Holm Mills and given on Home's map of 1774.

Bellachlan *Baile Lachlainn* Lachlan's steading/township. Also Balachlan. In the region of Mile End (Kinmylies).

Flora MacDonald gazes down on The Balloch (Am Bealach), the pass connecting Castle Street at left with View Place at right.

Bellahellich The meaning is uncertain but it is possibly *Baile na h-Èileig*, Township of the èileag. Close to Torvean and River Ness. An *èileag* is a "V"- shaped arrangement, open at both ends, into which deer were driven and shot with arrows as they came out the narrow end. An alternative is *Baile an Eilich*; *eileach* is a mill-race, embankment or bank of stones used to guide fish into a bag-net.

Brayrinchaltin *Bràigh Raon a' Challtainn* The upper part of the field of the hazel (trees). Formed part of the south-eastern boundary of the town lands in the 16th Century. Also called "Bruichmor-caltine" *(Bruach Mhòr a' Challtainn)*, the large bank of the hazels. Between Muckovie and Balvonie of Inshes.

Caiplich, The *A' Chaiplich* Place of horses ie horse pasture. High ground to the west of the town on which rights of pasturing and peat-cutting were granted by Royal Charter to the townsfolk.

Carneinwarrane *Càrn an Fhuarain* Cairn of the spring/well. One of the markers of the eastern boundary of the old town lands. See **Knocknacreich**. *approx 715439*

Horses in Inverness Place Names

There are three words meaning "horse" which commonly appear in Gaelic place names, and all are found in Inverness: *Capall* (the element in *A' Chaiplich*, place of horses) is related to the Latin *caballus* (from which the Spanish *caballo* is derived), and shares a common origin with the English *cavalier* and *cavalry*. It is also found in Inverness in *Capall-Innis* (Capel Inch), the horse island or meadow. *Marc*, from which the Gaelic word *marcachd* (riding) is derived, is found in *Marc-Innis* (Merkinch), while the standard modern word for horse, *each* (related to the Latin *equus* and English *equine*) is found in its possessive form *eich* in *Dail an Eich* (Dalneigh), field of the horse.

Clachan Donachy *Clachan Donnchaidh* Ostensibly Duncan's hamlet but possibly meaning the Robertsons' hamlet (*Clann Donnchaidh* being the Gaelic for Robertson), after local landowners. An old name for Culcabock village.

Cnoc na gobhar *Cnoc nan Gobhar* Hill of the goats. A knoll not far from Tomnahurich where goat-markets were once held.

Crèadh Innis see **Graidhe an Uisge**.

Culclachie Possibly *Cùil Clachaidh*, stone nook. According to Charles Fraser-Mackintosh this was the old name for Nairnside.

Fuaran a' Chragain Bhric The spring of the speckled rock. Sometimes called in English the Well of the Spotted Rock. In the vicinity of Craig Dunain. According to a paper of the Inverness Scientific Society and Field Club in 1878, this was considered to be a fairy well at which changelings could be exchanged back for the parents' own child. Another well in the vicinity was *Am Fuaran Dearg* (the red spring). The country surrounding Inverness was dotted with a vast number of wells and springs, all of which bore Gaelic names. Among them were *Fuaran na Làire Bàine* (the white mare's well) and *Fuaran na Ceapaich* (the Keppoch well), both at Culduthel, and *Fuaran a' Mhaighstir* at Leys, reputedly named after the Leys Bàrd, William Mackenzie, who was a schoolmaster there for forty years and who wrote of the well's sweet water. See also **Priseag Well**.

Glascarnenacreich *Glas Chàrn na Crìche* Grey boundary cairn. One of the eastern boundary markers of the ancient town lands. Near Muckovie at 714438.

Graidhe an Uisge The middle of the three scalps (mussel beds) historically sited at the mouth of the River Ness, also known in English as Middle Scalp. The name, which appears to mean "loved one of the water" has been given as a corruption of *Cridhe an Uisge,* "the heart or middle of the water", but it is more likely to be derived from *Crèadh-Innis* (clay island). See **Ronach, Scalp na Caorach** and **Scalp Phadruig Mhoir.**

Knockdow *An Cnoc Dubh* The black hill. To the east of Craig Phadrig, and south of Balnafettack, listed on Home's map of 1774. *approx. 644453*

Knockgur/Knock-na-gur *Cnoc a' Ghaorra* The hill of the gore. A site above Clachnaharry (in the vicinity of Woodside Crescent) which Cromwell's troops established as an abattoir. The name was still applied to a farm in the 1860s when the Ordnance Survey was mapping the area. *647463*

Knockintinnel *Cnoc an Tionail* Gathering or rallying hill. Listed as early as the 14th Century as Knokyntynole. This may have been a location where Invernessians would rally when required by the burgesses or forces of the Crown. It is now the site of Cameron Barracks. *679457*

Knocknakirk *Cnoc na Circe* Hill of the hen (possibly grouse). The old name for Upper Slackbuie. *673416*

Knoknacreich *Cnoc na Crìche* Hill of the boundary. An older name for *Càrn an Fhuarain* (see **Carneinwarrane**)

Knoknagad *Cnoc nan Gad* Hill of the withes. Old boundary marker of the town lands between Bogbain and Milton of Leys. Probably at *703423*.

Lagchaltin Presumably *Lag a' Challtainn* Hazel hollow. Recorded in the Burgh Records as part of the lands of Eister Inschis in 1629. The usual dialectal form of *lag* in Inverness is *slag*.

Machrie, The *A' Mhachraidh* A derivation of *machair*, a plain. Flat land now known as Raigmore.

Maggot (The) Part of the town close to the river, adjacent to the northern end of Church Street. The origin of the name is a mystery, and no separate Gaelic version of it exists today. Some authorities have claimed that the name was derived from St Margaret, as a chapel dedicated to that saint had once existed on the site, but it is worth noting that a flat area on the river bank in Nairn is also called the Maggot, and it may be that the word has an origin in the Gaelic "magh" (a plain, flat area). Given as Maggat on Home's map of 1774. A local strongman called "Jock on the Maggot" once carried *Clach na Cùdainn* to the top of the Old Jail stairs. *664456*

The Maggot (Maggat) as shown on Home's map of 1774. It was adjacent to the northern end of Church Street (Sràid na h-Eaglaise) *and an area long associated with the church which is known even today as The Glebe* (An Glìob)

Ouckmore Possibly *An t-Achadh mòr,* big field. Land adjacent to Muirtown, given on Home's map of 1774.

Polchro Possibly *Poll a' Chrò,* pool of the cruive (for catching salmon) or pool of the cattle-fold; Charles Fraser-Mackintosh gave it as Pool of the Cattle *(Poll a' Chruidh).* An old fishing pool on the River Ness to the south of **Polvanie**.

Polla Criadh *Poll Crèadha* The clay pit. A location on Telford Road now occupied by a shop but for many years the site of a nursery and garden centre. Approx. 656456.

Polvanie *Poll Bheathain* St. Bean's Pool (named after the saint whose name was given to Torvean and Kilvean). A favoured fishing pool to the west of the Ness Islands at approx. 663437, sometimes called "Polvanie Shott". The other fishings were called by a mixture of Gaelic and English names: Cherry Shott, Friar's Shott (a name still in use), Island Shott, Silver Pool, Trot Shott, Pol Bhàn (*Am Poll Bàn,* fair or clear-bottomed pool) and Poul-malie (meaning unclear).

Priseag Well *Fuaran na Priseig* Well or spring of the small thicket. Close to the bridge on the Beauly Road at Clachnaharry. Said to have been blessed by St. Kessock, its water was used to treat sore eyes. If the water were silvered before drinking, as with a crooked sixpence, it was reputed to act against the effects of the evil eye. *644465*

Pusag *Pusag* Kitten/pussy. The name of a spout of water at Clachnaharry which was at one time the main water supply for the village. The Ordnance Survey records of 1868-70 relate the story that the name was transferred from a nearby public-house of the same name when that establishment lost its licence. Apparently this allowed locals to talk in public about going to the "Pusag", even though they often meant the illegally-trading tavern rather than the water source!

Ronach *An Rònach* Place of seals. The westernmost of the scalps at the mouth of the River Ness, also called West Scalp (see **Scalp na Caorach**). These banks were important for the local people as mussel beds, but were a danger to shipping and were thus modified. Ronach was uncovered only at low spring tides, at which times seals would haul up on it.

Sabhal Daraich, An The oak barn. An ancient building behind the West Church which was reputed to have been built by the fairies of Tomnahurich and which was strictly avoided after nightfall.

Scalp na Caorach *Scalp nan Caorach* The shellfish bed/shingly bank of the sheep. The flat area below high water on the shore of the firth between the river mouth and the Kessock Bridge. *Scalp* most likely came into the local Gaelic from the Scots *scaup* or possibly from Norse sources, as the word is of Scandinavian origin. It designates a flat area of the shore or offshore shoal, particularly where shellfish can be collected at low tide, and is equivalent to the Gaelic *oitir*, although it is the loan-word which seems to have had prominence in the Gaelic of Inverness. The Ordnance Survey compilers of 1868-70 claim that this scalp was once covered with grass and grazed by sheep, and it is recorded that cattle fed on the scalps at the mouth of the River Ness. However, it is possible that the name is a corruption of *Scalp na Curaich,* the scalp of the leather boat. The names of these scalps were all still in common use in the 19th century. See **Ronach, Graidh an Uisge** and **Scalp Phadruig Mhoir.**

Scatgate The old name for the road that led from Academy Street to the Longman before 19th Century renaming and modern developments turned it into the vestigial Rose Street *(Sràid an Ròsaich)*. In the 19th Century the colloquial name among Inverness Gaels was *Sràid na Croiche* (the gibbet street) because it led out to the site of the public hangings, which were large events in those days. But, although a mixed Gaelic/Scots origin has been postulated for Scatgate (meaning "herring road" as that was the route along which fish landed by Black Isle fishermen would come to market in Inverness), it is more likely that this is an example of a Scots name of partial Norse origin, as *scat* was a form of tax or tribute levied on communities under Scandinavian rule; the name, which is recorded as early as the 14th Century, therefore meant "tax road" (the tax on the fishermen's landings). *666456*

Scalp Phadruig Mhoir *Scalp Phàdraig Mhòir* Big Peter's scalp. The easternmost of the scalps at the mouth of the River Ness, close to the south side of Kessock Bridge. A favoured spot for mussel-collecting, but only visible at the spring tides. The identity of *Pàdraig Mòr* is unknown. See **Ronach, Graidhe an Uisge** and **Scalp na Caorach.**

Scriodan-sgràd The old name for Stoneyfield (692458), reportedly well known in the earlier part of the 19th Century. The second element is cryptic, but the name is obviously connected with the nearby Scretan Burn *(Allt an Sgrìodain)*. *Sgrìodan* means a stony ravine.

Travelling people at Stoneyfield (Scriodan-sgràd), possibly in the 1930s. The travellers have a special place in the cultural life of the Highlands and have been visiting Inverness for centuries. Of all the social groups in the eastern Highlands, this was the one which remained most loyal to the Gaelic language and its traditions in the 20th Century. The last great traditional Gaelic storytellers in the eastern Highlands are travelling people who learned their stories in the tent or by the campfire.

Slag nam Mèirleach Thieves' hollow. A notorious spot, near the junction of the Stratherrick and Holm roads, where muggers of the 18th Century would lie in wait for travellers. Given as *Slochd nam Mèirleach* by 20th Century authors but as *Slacknamarlach* by a knowledgeable local in the 19th Century which seems to settle the issue in favour of *slag* (which is more appropriate for the topography). There appears to have been no English form of the name. Probably the dell at 650421.

Slochd Dunache *Sloc Dhonnchaidh* Duncan's hollow or dell. This appears to have been an alternative name for King Duncan's Grave (also known as King Duncan's Hollow) next to the Culcabock roundabout. The *Donnchadh* referred to may be the local Robertson family *(Clann Donnchaidh)*, rather than the ancient king of Scotland. *682448*

Stac an Fhithich Raven's rock. On east side of Dunain Hill. Two other precipices nearby were called *An Stac Meadhanach* (middle) and *An Stac Beag* (small). Below them was *Am Poll Cruaidh* (the hard bog).

Toberdonich *Tobar Dòmhnaich* Well of the Lord. One of the old boundary markers of the town lands. In region of Lower Muckovie.

Tom na Ceann *Tom nan Ceann* Hill of the heads. A site of beheadings when this method of execution was employed in Inverness. Now occupied by Ardkean Tower at the corner of Culduthel and Old Edinburgh Roads. Also called Barnhill, the Gaelic name was still in general use in the latter half of the 18th Century. The road to this site (ie Castle Street, *Sràid a' Chaisteil*) was at one time called Doomsdale Street. *667448*

Tore more *An Tòrr Mòr* The big mound. In the region of Scorguie Road, given on Home's map of 1774. Close-by was **Tore beag** *(An Tòrr Beag* - the small mound) and the cryptic, but almost certainly Gaelic, *Cretnapirach*.

Poachers from the Inverness area in the second half of the 19th Century. One of these three worthies, known as Dunk Culloden or "the heckler", is mentioned in John Fraser's "Reminiscences of Inverness". Rural characters from Inverness's hinterland, largely Gaelic-speaking until the 20th Century, regularly appeared on the streets and in the shops (not to mention the court and jail!) of the town, contributing to its colour and diversity over the centuries. Some of them settled in the town.

Place Names Still in Use

The following are names of places or objects in and around Inverness, most of which are anglicised forms of Gaelic originals and which remain in use today. In a few cases, they are translations of the original Gaelic. Some names of non-Gaelic origin, a few of which have a Gaelic form, are also included. Modern orthography is employed for all Gaelic forms of the names where the modern standard conflicts with the original. The six-numbered grid references are for the local Ordnance Survey maps (Explorer 416 or Landranger 26 and 27).

Abban (The) *An t-Àban* The backwater or disused/silted-up channel. The name is preserved in Abban Street *(Sràid an Àbain)*. Some authors have suggested that it is a corrupted form of *abhainn* (river), or *òban* (creek) but these are incorrect. Home's map of 1774 shows a "salt water lake" called the "Nabon" backing up into the area now occupied by Abban Street. Sometime prior to that the "Abban" was one of the outlets in the Ness River delta. During a street-development programme on the western side of the river in 1870, the Abban was filled in with the surplus rock and soil, and then built upon. The responsible architect, Alexander Ross, wrote that he had "the river outlet over the roadway at Huntly Place to the Abban raised, and the river stopped from passing to the sea by this route." The Ordnance Survey map of 1871 erroneously gave Abban Street as "Abbey Street" though this was changed to the correct name in the 1905 edition. A flat area close to the Abban was called Dalnabon *(Dail an Àbain,* the Field or Dale of the Abban). Professor Watson considered *àban* to be restricted to the Inverness locality, the word also being applied historically to a small creek off Loch Dochfour and another on the shoreline at Petty. The Inverness *àban* is at 660456.

Allanfearn *An t-Àilean Feàrna* The alder meadow. Near Culloden. *717475.*

Alturlie *Allt Rolaidh,* recorded as Alt-Terly by Pont at the end of the 16th Century. There is however no burn *(allt)* there, and this supports Watson's conjecture that the name was originally Ard-rolaidh *(Àird Rolaidh),* *àird* meaning a prominent high point as occurs in this locality (at 715495). The meaning of *rolaidh* is unknown. Nearby Brecknish is *Breac-Innis,* the speckled meadow.

Aultnaskiach/Ault na Skiah *Allt nan Sgitheach*. Burn of the hawthorns. First recorded as Auldnaskiahe in 1592 and Altnaskiach in 1595. Flows into the Ness downstream from the islands at *665441*.

Ballifeary *Baile na Faire*. Township of the sentinel or watch. A place west of the river where sentinels would be posted to give warning to the townsfolk of the approach of a hostile force from the west or south-west. One of Inverness's oldest attested place names, with a record (as *Balnafare*) in 1244. Given on Home's map of 1774, (below) as Baliferie. *662442*

Balloan *Baile an Lòin*. Township of the small loch. This seems the most likely interpretation as, according to the Ordnance Survey work of the late 1860s, there had at one time been a loch there before the area was drained (it was there in the mid-18th Century). An alternative meaning of *lòn* is a marsh or a stream with marshy banks which would fit the landscape adjacent to Balloan Road. It was a notably marshy place and is still prone to flooding. *671427*

Balloch *Baile an Loch* Township of the loch. *735471*. Non Gaelic-speakers are often intrigued as to why the second syllable of this name is emphasised, whereas the Balloch close to Loch Lomond is pronounced with the emphasis on the first syllable. The reason lies in the Gaelic original. The southern Balloch is *Bealach* (pass) in which the first syllable is emphasised. In the Inverness Balloch, the *loch* element is emphasised. Feabuie close to Balloch is *An Fhèith Bhuidhe* (the yellow bog).

Baile in Inverness Place Names

The word *baile*, anglicised in names as *Bal-, Ball-, Balli-, Bell-* and *Bella-* (and commonly *Bally-* in Ireland) is a term which in modern usage can represent a settlement as small as a farm *(baile-fearainn)* or as large as a metropolis *(baile mòr/cathair-bhaile)*. The City of Inverness is known as *Baile Inbhir Nis* or *Cathair-bhaile Inbhir Nis*. It is also one of the name elements most diagnostic of Gaelic settlement in Scotland, being found even in the border counties and Lothian, and being relatively common in Dumfries and Galloway, in addition to the Highlands and Islands (except in Orkney and Shetland). In Inverness most *baile* names would originally represent farm steadings or a group of dwellings in close association. It was often translated into English as "town", abbreviated to "ton". Thus, in Inverness, *Baile a' Chnuic* (hill-town) became Hilton, *Baile a' Mhuilinn* (mill-town) became Milton, and *Baile an Fhraoich* (literally heather-town) became Muirton (moor-town).

Balmore (of Leys) *Am Baile Mòr, Baile Mòr Leigheis* The big township. 668407

Balnacraig *Baile na Creige* Township of the rock. Close to Dunain at *632431*.

Balnafettack *Baile nam Feadag.* Near Scorguie. Considered by Watson to mean "township of the plovers". Listed as Balnafetic on John Home's 1774 Map of Inverness, when it was a farm. *643453*

Balnagaig *Baile na Gàig* Township of the cleft, named for a gap in the ridge behind the farm. Also Balnagaick. Near Dunain at 636429.

Balnakyle *Baile na Coille* Township of the wood. Now part of the suburb of **Lochardil**, the name is preserved in Balnakyle Road.

Balphadrig *Baile Phàdraig* Peter/Patrick's steading/township. South of Kinmylies. *643437*.

Balrobert *Baile Raibeirt* Robert's steading/township. To the south of the city at 653397.

Balvonie (of Inshes) *Baile a' Mhonaidh* Township of the hill or rough grazing. 698431.

Beauly Firth *Linne Fharair* in Gaelic, the English name relates to the village of Beauly at the head of the firth. The name is French (*Beau Lieu*, beautiful place), bestowed on the Priory of Beauly by its Norman founders. *Farar* was the original Gaelic name for the Beauly River (which is still known as the River Farrar in its upper reaches). The village of Beauly in Gaelic is *A'Mhanachainn* (the monastery) or *Manachainn 'ic Shimidh* (Lovat's monastery). Another old name for the Beauly Firth was *Poll an Ròid*.

Black Isle, The *An t-Eilean Dubh* Not actually an island but a peninsula – a feature often referred to as "island" in various European languages. It is often presumed that the English is a translation of the Gaelic and it has been postulated that the *dubh* refers to the one-time uncultivated nature of the peninsula, a fact confirmed by the compilers of the Old Statistical Account who said it was four-fifths black moor in their day. Some scholars have claimed that the Gaelic is a corruption of *Eilean Dubhthaich* (St Duthac's Isle); medieval pilgrimages to the saint's "town" at *Baile Dhubhthaich* (Tain) were made from the south through the Black Isle. Older names for the peninsula were Ardmeanach (*An Àird Mheadhanach*, the mid-height – between the two firths) and Eddirdail (given as *Eadar-Dhà-Dhail*, "between two dales", but more likely derived from *Eadar-Dhà-Dhobhair*, "between two waters").

Bogbain W. J. Watson, who knew this settlement when it was occupied by indigenous Gaelic-speakers, considered it to be *Am Bog Bàn*, the fair bog, so called because of the bog cotton which grew there. He gave *Am Bac Bàn* for Bogbain in Easter Ross. The A9 to the south of the city passes through Bogbain. *706427*

Founder of Bogbain Adventure and Heritage Farm on the outskirts of Inverness, Liza Mulholland – here with son Roddy – welcomes visitors to a development which gives Gaelic and English equal prominence in its signage. "The family at this farm in the early part of the 20th Century were all first-language Gaelic speakers from this area," says Liza, "and we wanted to show people that Gaelic is still alive, and to encourage them to use it."

Bught, The Historically the Gaelic name was *Cill Bheathain* (see **Kilvean**) but modern Gaels refer to *Am Bucht* and to Bught Park (at 662440) as *Pàirc a' Bhucht*, with the "u" pronounced after the English fashion. It has been suggested that Bught is derived from the Gaelic *bochd* (see **Diriebught**) but this appears erroneous. It is most likely a Scots word, designating an enclosure for sheep or pigs. It is first recorded as Buthe in 1443 and Buch in 1449. Bught Park is today one of Scotland's premier locations for the playing of shinty, the ancient sport of the Gael. One of the Inverness Club's most successful seasons was in 1951-52 when they won the Camanachd Cup Final in Glasgow in front of a crowd of over ten thousand.

Cairnlaw Locality through which flows Cairnlaw Burn near Milton of Culloden. Rights were granted to the burgesses of Inverness over the "Carn Laws" in the Great (or Golden) Charter of 1591. It has been suggested that the name originated from *Car an Là* (the turn of the day) because of a change of fortune during a battle in ancient times. This is dubious but the name appears to be so old that its origin is now lost. *703463*

Caisteal Rollach *Caisteal Rolach* A pure Gaelic name, representing what is now an oval stone enclosure between Leys and Bogbain. *Caisteal* means "castle" (both words are derived from from the Latin *castellum*), but the meaning of *rollach* is obscure. *694408*

Caledonian Canal The name, of course, dates only from the early 19th Century and is English in origin, although many Gaelic-speakers were engaged in the canal's construction. In Gaelic it is *An Canàl Cailleannach*.

Capel Inch *Capall-Innis* Mare or horse island or meadow. When part of the river Ness flowed through the Abban, this low lying area was an island, possibly flooded at times and most likely covered in grasses; and it is probably a place where horses were grazed in a convenient location close to, but outside, the original town. The name is thought to be old, predating the holding of horse sales there in the 19th century. Dwelly's dictionary tells us that the old meaning of *capall* was a "horse broken to the bit" and it may be that this distinguished it from the nearby **Merkinch**, also a grazing ground for horses. *662463.*

Carnarc Point In today's Gaelic this point at the west side of the mouth of the Ness (at 660473) is equivalent to the English ie *Càrnarc* or *Gob Chàrnairc*, the original meaning having been lost because of the "very remote antiquity of the name", as the Old Statistical Account of 1791 has it. There was a cairn built there (where a beacon now exists) to warn shipping of the river mouth – which may account for the first part of the name, but the second element remains a puzzle. Suggestions include "Cairn of the Sea" *(Càrn Fhairge?)* and "Cairn of Hardship or Danger" *(Càrn Airc)*. The outstanding 19th Century architect, later Provost of Inverness, Alexander Ross, was of the opinion that it had anciently housed a crannog (Gaelic *crannag*), a water-dwelling erected

Carnarc Point at the mouth of the River Ness: a cairn of danger?

on an artificial island, of which there were a number along the Beauly Firth, and it is a possibility that Carnarc is simply a corruption of the Gaelic *Crannag*. Set against that is the name of a definite crannog near Bunchrew, still visible at low spring tides, which also bears *càrn* in its name – *an Càrn Dubh* (the black cairn).

Carse, The *A' Chars.* The original word is Scots, which passed into Gaelic as a loan-word. It means flat land adjacent to water and refers to the ground to the west of the river mouth. *653464*

Castle Heather *Caisteal na Lethoir* Castle of the slope or border. The modern English name is a corruption of the earlier Castle Leather or Castle Leathers, and has no connection with the famous plant which covers much of the Highlands. According to the Old Statistical Account of 1793, the original was "Caistal nan leoirach" meaning the "castle of the recluse or retired" but this appears unlikely. Indeed "castle of the slope" fits perfectly the location of the ancient earthworks thought to have given the name to the site. W. J. Watson claimed the modern English name appeared in print as early as 1758 but the Ordnance Survey of 1866-7 gave it as Castleleathers. The earliest records are as Castletoun de Lafere in 1508 and Castle Lathir in 1537. *680427*

Castle Hill *Tom a' Chaisteil* Hillock of the castle. The site of Inverness Castle. The English and Gaelic names have co-existed for many centuries. *666452*

Castlehill (of Inshes) *Caisteal Still,* Castle of the strip (of land). The English is a corruption of the Gaelic. *698443*

Cauldeen Burn Probably *Allt a' Challtainn* Hazel burn. The name is now perpetuated in a road and primary school. *670427*

Chapel Yard A cemetery, at the northern end of the old town centre, on ground with ancient links to the church. A variety of Gaelic names are in currency – *Cladh a' Chaibeil* and *Cladh an t-Seipeil* being most common (both meaning "cemetery of the chapel"). It is unclear as to whether the Gaelic or English was the original. I suspect the English, as Seumas MacBheathain in a book of Gaelic spiritual poetry and elegies to religious figures published in Inverness in 1880 wrote, "tha uaigh san t-Cheipal-Gheard" (his grave is in the Chapel Yard) in which the unconventional Gaelic name seems simply to echo the English one. The graveyard of the High Church was historically called *An Cladh Mòr* (the big or great cemetery) in Gaelic. *665457*

Charleston *Baile Theàrlaich* Charles's steading/township. Now part of the suburb of Kinmylies (641434). Charlestown in North Kessock (643483), also *Baile Theàrlaich* in Gaelic, was named for Charles Mackenzie, Laird of Kilcoy, who died in 1813.

Cherry, The The part of the River Ness between Capel Inch and the Harbour. The name, while not as familiar to local people today as it would have been to previous generations, is still shown on many maps. It is generally thought to be Gaelic in origin but, if so, the meaning is cryptic. *Curach* (hide-covered boat) and *sè-ràmhach* (six-oared galley) are among the suggestions; the flat ground at the mouth of the river, where such craft might have been hauled on shore, was called the Churryflat (1365). It might also be noted that Balcherry in Easter Ross originated as *Baile a' Cheathraimh,* town of the quarter (davoch). But in Inverness the name originally applied, not to a part of the river itself, but to a wall or the ground adjacent to a wall, probably made of stone, which protected the town lands from the high tidal waters of the firth

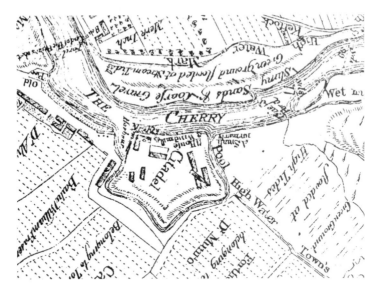

(the building of houses and middens between the dyke and the sea was actually forbidden in the 17th Century). The Inverness Burgh Records of ca.1556 describe "the ald dyke alias Churre" and in 1576 the Burgh Court Books give an account of "the dyke that lyis to the Churrie at the North"; in 1240 and again in 1530 it is given as Scurry and The Scurrie respectively. It is shown as Town's Dyke (with The Cherry in its current position on the river) on Home's map of 1774 (see illustrations). The modern Gaelic is *An Tearaidh* (as the English) but it is just possible that its origin lies anciently in *An Tiùrr*, the part of a shore where seaweed is cast up by the highest tides – the exact location where the "Churrie dyke" was built by the townsfolk to protect their lands. *663462*

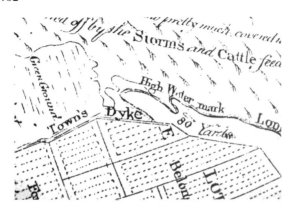

Clachnacuddin *Clach na Cùdainn* Stone of the tub (see illustration p.4). A flat-topped stone now located on a pedestal outside the Town House (not exactly its original location, although close to it), it was reputedly the place where water-carriers and clothes-washers ferrying their loads to and from the river would rest their tubs to engage in an exchange of gossip and pleasantries. While largely ignored by the populace today (the young men no longer linger to chat up the women there), it was long beloved of Invernessians and considered something of a palladium for the town (Inverness men who travelled the world often referred to themselves as "Clachnacuddin Boys"). Tradition has it that the stone originated in Lochalsh where it was employed in the installation of the Lords of the Isles

Clach na Cùdainn and Queen Victoria: Crowds celebrate the Queen's Diamond Jubilee outside the Inverness Town House on 22 June 1897. Draped across the front of the building is a banner in Gaelic - "Fhad 's a mhaireas Clach na Cùdainn, mairidh cliù Victoria air chuimhne" (As long as Clachnacuddin exists, Victoria's fame will be remembered)

as Lords of Lochalsh. Before being encased, as it currently is, John Maclean, the "Clachnacuddin Nonagenarian" tells us that a strong local worthy known as Jock on the Maggot (after his place of dwelling) carried the stone to the top of the Old Jail stairs but was unable to move it from there; another broad-shouldered townsman of the name of Maclean then returned it to its rightful place next to the market cross. This seems to run counter to the suggestion by Murdoch MacIntosh, Sheriff Clerk and President of the Inverness Scientific Society and Field Club, who claimed in 1948 that the stone had been endowed in older times with the utmost of respect because of a religious significance, and that it was associated with baptism, not the washing of clothes (unless the ancient respect had been forgotten by the time that Jock on the Maggot came along). Given as Clach-na-Cutin in English in a book in 1811, the town's fathers rejected this anglicised form in favour of Clachnacuddin. The name is perpetuated in a local football team. *667452*

Clachnahagaig This is a fascinating and ancient name relating to a stone between Torvean and the River Ness which has for long been a marker of the southern boundary of the town's rights over fishings (and other aspects of land use). Even today, members of the local angling club are told that their permit allows them to "angle with rod and line on both banks of the River Ness from Clachnahagaig Stone to the sea..." However, it is only the position of the original stone which is marked today, as the stone itself was removed during the building of the Caledonian Canal. And there is much debate over the exact name of the original and its meaning. In the Golden Charter of 1591, King James VI granted the burgesses of the town "the waters of the Ness on both sides from Clachnagaick to the sea, with all fishings..." The stone (or perhaps another one nearby) also appears in the records as Clachnachaggag, Clachnahalig, Clachnahelig, Clachnahielet and Clachnahulaig. William Mackay in 1913 reckoned *Clach na h-Eagaig* (*stone of the little cleft*) to be most likely, but in truth we shall probably never know its original meaning.

Clachnaharry *Clach na h-Aithrigh* Stone of repentance or penance; later the name of the village that was developed near the stone. This name has been the subject of much misinformed comment, being given variously as *Clach na h-Eithre* (stone of the boat), *Clach na Faire* and *Clach na h-Aire* (the watch stone), and *Clach na h-Àirigh* (the shieling stone).

The earliest written record, however, gives the game away. In the Wardlaw Manuscript (1666-1700) the Rev. James Fraser tells us *"The battle of Clach-ni-Harry ie. the Repentance or Pennance Stone happened June 27 1378."* The word *aithrigh* is now obsolete in Scottish Gaelic but still exists in Irish. The Repentance or Penance would probably have been conducted, in the days when Catholicism held sway, after confession, consisting of the repetition of a given number of paternosters in the vicinity of the stone. *647463*

Cradlehall This has no Gaelic connection. It is reputedly named after a cradle, attached to a block and tackle, in the home of 18th Century road-builder William Caulfeild, by which drunken guests could be hoisted to their upstairs bedrooms! *703448*

Craig Phadrig (Creag Phàdraig) from above the city's roofs

Craig Phadrig *Creag Phàdraig* Peter's or Patrick's rock. A high point overlooking Inverness from the west, thought by many to be the site of the fort of King Brude of the Picts. This is lent credence by the preferred Gaelic name of local folk as recorded in 1822 – *Làrach an Taigh Mhòir* (the site of the great house). Recorded on the Register of the Great Seal in 1592 as Craigfadrick. Sadly, the eponymous Pàdraig remains unidentified. *640453*

Craigton *Baile na Creige* township/steading of the rock. At north side of Kessock Bridge. *660482*

Crown, The *An Crùn* This name was in common colloquial usage by the start of the 19th Century, but it seems to be English and is unlikely to have any ancient Gaelic heritage. It was formerly called Auld Castlehill or MacBeth's Castlehill. *672454*

Culcabock *Cùil na Càbaig* This name, originally a location in the vicinity of where the Inverness Golf Club now has its course (referred to colloquially as Culcabock Golf Course), is recorded as Culkabok and Culcabok in the Inverness Burgh Records of 1556-61 and as Coulchabarck on Pont's map of ca. 1585-1595. The Gaelic, as given by W. J. Watson, is *Cùil na Càbaig* (nook of the cheese or kebbock), which accords with local tradition, although the reason for the appellation remains a mystery. *680444*

Culduthel *Cùil Daothuil* Recorded as Culdutheld and Culduthellis on the Register of the Great Seal (1642) and sometimes erroneously given as *Cùl-du-thuil* (the back of the dark stream) in Gaelic, the first element of this name is the common Gaelic word *cùil*, meaning "nook"; the second is *daothail*, of which the meaning is unknown, although it is likely of the same origin as the parish name (Duthil) in Strathspey. This was confirmed by W. J Watson and is attested by the song, *Òran do Chornailfhear Seumas Friosal, Chuldaothal* (song for Col. James Fraser of Culduthel) which was included in a collection of Gaelic songs published in Inverness in 1806. The name applies to an area east of the Ness, on the southern edge of the city (the old Culduthel Hospital is at 665423) and is perpetuated in Culduthel Road *(Rathad Chùil Daothail)*.

Cùil in Inverness Place Names

The element *cùil*, anglicised in place names as Cul-, Cull- or Coul-, and meaning a "nook", occurs in several localities in the Inverness-Black Isle area (examples from the Black Isle include Culbokie and Coulmore). It is easily confused with another Gaelic word *cùl*, which also appears in place names, meaning the "back of something". The diagnostic difference, if not apparent from the landscape, is the quality of the "u" and the terminal "l". This, of course, can only be determined where the Gaelic name is known and used by Gaelic-speakers indigenous to the area. Thankfully, scholars like W. J. Watson were still able to access information from native speakers who belonged to Inverness and its environs. Watson considered all three major Inverness Cul- names to be derived from *cùil*, rather than *cùl*.

Cullernie Meaning uncertain but possibly *Cùil Àirne* Nook of the sloe. Listed as Coulerny on Pont's Map of 1585-95. *734475*

Culloden *Cùil Lodair* The nook of the small pool/marsh. The name is, of course, famous worldwide because of the battle in 1746, and it is an unusual one because the ancient Gaelic is more faithfully represented today in the anglicised form than it is in the modern Gaelic, in which a terminal "r" has replaced the original "n". It is recorded as Cullodyn and Cullodyne in the Inverness Burgh Records of 1556-61 and as Coulloddinn on Pont's map of ca. 1585-1595. Despite wild and various speculation on its origins over the last 150 years or so, it is clearly identifiable as *Cùil Lodain*. There is an Achloddan (*Achadh Lodain*, field of the little pool) in Strathnairn. However, the modern Gaelic form is found as early as the 18th Century, as in the poem about the battle, *Latha Chuilodair*, by the famous Jacobite soldier-poet, John Roy Stewart. Both the battlefield at 745451 and the battle itself are known in Gaelic as *Blàr Chùil Lodair*, the context informing the listener as to what is meant. Close to Culloden is Viewhill Farm which was the subject of a place name dispute in the 1860s when the tenant farmer wanted to supplant the old name

of Drumbuie (*An Druim Buidhe*, the yellow ridge) with View Hill, a move that
was opposed by the proprietor, Arthur Forbes. The tenant obviously won the
battle.

Dalcross Often erroneously referred to as *Dail Chrois* in Gaelic today, the
original and correct Gaelic is *Dealganros* (prickly point or prickly wood).
Indeed, an older English form of the name was Delginross. It is a little bit
outside the geographical scope of this book but is included as it is the site of
Inverness Airport. Nearby Ardersier is *Àird nan Saor*, the promontory of the
carpenters, although Professor Watson remained open to the possibility that
the origin of the second element was *saothair*, a low promontory covered
with water at high tide.

Dalneigh *Dail an Eich* Field of the horse. The original was for a long time
faithfully reflected in the English speech of Invernessians who pronounced
it "Dalneich" well into the 20th Century. Indeed, that is how it was recorded
on the first Ordnance Survey map of 1871. However later cartographers gave
it as Dalneigh and it is listed as such by Alexander Mackenzie in 1884 (see
illustration next page). The orthography has ensured the demise of the older
form of the name so that it is now generally pronounced "dal-NAY", although
the original Gaelic name is still widely used by Gaelic-speakers. *654448*

Can cartographers accelerate a loss of heritage? Dalneich in the first Ordnance Survey map (above, left) was replaced by Dalneigh in the second edition (above right). In a literate society, the old (and meaningful) names, handed down by oral tradition, can soon become forgotten.

Dalreoch *An Dail Riabhach* The brindled field. At Lower Dunain. *630416*

Daviot *Deimhidh* in Gaelic, but the name is probably originally Pictish, meaning "strong place" because of its hill fort. Recorded as Deveth in 1234 and as Devy by Pont in the late 16th Century. *725407* Dores (*Duras* in Gaelic) is another local place name which might have originated with the Picts, bearing a similar meaning to Daviot, although Professor Watson latterly considered it to be from the Gaelic *Dubh-ros*, Black wood.

Diriebught Generally thought to be *Doire nam Bochd,* meaning Grove of the poor, but this appears to be based on a single reference from 1795 in which Provost Inglis referred to it as "*Dire na Pouchk,* or the Land of the Poor". *Tìr nam Bochd,* land of the poor, has been suggested as an alternative. Reported to have been given by Sir Robert Chisholm of Chisholm to the Church in Inverness in 1362 as a gift to the poor of the parish. In Provost Inglis's day the name referred to a field in the

vicinity of Millburn Academy (677457). The earliest reference is to Deyrbowchte in 1376, and Pont's map of ca.1585-95 gives it as Deirbocht, very much in its current recognised location. The name is preserved in Diriebught Road.

Dochgarroch *Dabhach Gairbheach* The davoch of rough ground. The *davoch* is an ancient land measure which appears to have Pictish origins and there are several instances around Inverness in which this element is mixed with a Gaelic one eg Dochfour (*Dabhach Phùir,* davoch of good pasture), Dochnacraig

(*Dabhach na Creige*, davoch of the rock), Dochnalurig (*Dabhach na Luirg*, davoch of the narrow ridge). It appears likely that the internal "bh" in dabhach was not pronounced in the local Gaelic dialect as there are records of Daach na burg and Daacharn in ca. 1600.

Drakies The Gaelic is *Dreigidh*, but the meaning is unknown and it is possibly a name of Pictish origin. It is recorded as Drekeis in 1369, but it appears throughout recorded history with and without the terminal "s". Pont's map of ca. 1585-95 gives two adjacent locations called Dregy and it appears that this must be the reason for the "s" – it is simply a pluralisation (ie The Drakies), a common enough phenomenon in Scottish place names. This is supported by the occurrence of Drakye and Lytill Draky in the Inverness Burgh Records of 1556-61, and of Dreygie Moir *(ie Dreigidh Mòr)* and Dregy Beg *(Dreigidh Beag)* on a map drawn up ca. 1600. Inverness folklore has it that the name was connected to the Druids of old, being a corruption of the Gaelic *draoidh*, but this appears to be spurious. Now the name of a housing scheme. Drakies School is at 682442.

Pictish, Scots and Norse

While Gaelic forms the major strand in the place names of Inverness and its environs, other languages also made their contributions. The oldest, Pictish, gave us names which date back to at least 700 AD and may be considerably older than that. Examples are *aber* (the Pictish equivalent to *inver*) in Abriachan, *davach* or *doch* (eg Dochfour), Deimhidh (Daviot, "Strong Place") and Dreigidh (Drakies, meaning unknown). The diagnostic Pictish settlement element, *pit*, is found close to Inverness in Pitlundie (Black Isle) and Petty (place of "pits"). A later strand arrived with Scots-speakers, probably following the creation of the Royal Burgh, and are represented in names like Bught, Carse, Haugh and Holm (the last three of which passed into Gaelic as loan-words). The Norse, while having a major influence on the modern nomenclature of northern Scotland and contributing many loan-words to Gaelic, left virtually nothing that is incontestably theirs on the map of Inverness.

Drumbuie *An Druim Buidhe* Yellow ridge. Near Muckovie at 716439

Drumdevan *An Druim Dìomhain,* the idle or uncultivated ridge. See **Drummond**.

Drummond *Druiminn* W.J. Watson gave this as meaning "at or on the ridge", and it applies to a ridge which runs parallel to the Ness (approx. 668436). He and other authorities maintained that the original was *An Druim Dìomhain* (the idle i.e. uncultivated ridge), anglicised as Drumdevan, although there is another Drumdevan to the immediate south of the city at 665413. There is a Drumdivan near Dornoch which is of the same origin, and there are two places called Drumdeevin in Counties Donegal and Limerick. In the Irish instances, the "idle ridge" was a site for local amusements and pastimes.

Drumossie *Druim Athaisidh* The ridge of Ashie (of the worn-out pasture). Drumossie Moor runs from SW to NE to the east of Inverness and contains the Culloden Battlefield. It was given as Drim Ashey Moor in about 1750 and as "Drimmashie or Drumossie moor" in 1846. Much legend has attached itself to Ashie, namely that he was a Scandinavian Prince who was defeated here in battle by Fionn Mac Cumhail (Fingal) and his warriors, but the truth is likely to be more prosaic. W. J. Watson explained that Loch Ashie (630350) is *Loch Aithisidh,* originally *Loch Ath-innse,* the loch of the worn-out meadow ie of poor pasture, and that the ridge took its name from the loch. However, just to confuse matters slightly, there is also a small moor still called Drumashie Moor on the west side of the loch, and a good distance from the extensive Drumossie Moor, which lies to its east. The name is perpetuated in Drumossie Avenue in the Drakies estate.

Dunain *Dùn Eun* Hill or fort of birds. Recorded in English as Dunnane in 1568, it was reported to be "pronounced in three syllables by Gaelic-speaking people" (Inverness Scientific Society, 1917), and was given in 1821 as *Dun-eun.* The pronunciation, if not the etymology, is supported by Màiri Mhòr nan Òran's reference to *Dun-ian* in her poetry. The old hospital of Craig Dunain (*Creag Dhùn Eun* i.e. the rock of Dunain) is at 637438.

Essich *Easaich* Place of waterfalls. This locality, south of the city, was once known as *Fearann nan Ceann* (Land of the Heads), a name which can be dated to the mid-16ᵗʰ Century, according to the Clachnacuddin Nonagenarian. He tells the tale of a Laird of Mackintosh in 1550 who had offended the Earl of Huntly and whose punishment was to be beheaded at Strathbogie. In order to buy peace with the incensed Mackintoshes, Huntly was obliged to cede to them the lands of Essich in compensation. It was found out that the Mackintosh Laird had been betrayed to Huntly by one of his kinsmen, a Lachlan Mackintosh, who was then put to death by the clan. *647395*

Fluke Inn A plaque on the wall of this inn at Culcabock says the unusual name derives from the fact that the building once housed a fish market, but this is open to debate. There is a strong tradition that the name derives from the Gaelic *fliuch* (wet). The road on which the inn stands was once called Fluke Street as it led to the ford across a burn called Aultmurnoche or Altmuniack (probably *Allt Muineach*, thorny burn). *682446*

Fuaran Allt an Ionnlaid Well of the washing burn. Once a celebrated Inverness landmark, this spring in Muirtown, reputedly the haunt of both druid and priest in olden times, is now unkempt and overgrown. See p 76. *651461*

Fuaran a' Chlèirich Well or spring of the cleric (priest). An ancient well at Balloch (733472) now surrounded by a housing scheme. The roads and avenues nearby bear the name "Wellside" and the well has been retained as a feature surrounded by stone, but there is nothing to indicate its significance, and it has become heavily polluted by cans, bottles and other litter. See **Culloden Wells** p.77.

Fuaran a' Chladaich Spring of the shore. Below the high tide mark in the Beauly Firth at Bunchrew, this spring was frequented by Invernessians during cholera outbreaks, in the belief that its water would be unpolluted.

Haugh, The Flat land by the riverside, at 666445. From an old Scots word *halche,* and mentioned in William the Lion's charter of 1180. This word became the Gaelic *talchan*, and the locality is still called *An Talchan* in Gaelic. When Gaelic absorbed a Teutonic word starting with "h", it usually inserted an initial "t" (see **Holm**). Interestingly, the Gaelic name retains the original "l" which has disappeared from the modern word in Scots.

Fuaran Allt an Ionnlaid

The sorry state of the "well of the washing burn", which stands in an unkempt piece of ground adjacent to Clachnaharry Road at Muirtown, is a reflection on the changing values of Invernessians and the weakening of the townsfolk's connection with their ancient and unique traditions. This was once a famous Inverness landmark, sometimes known in English as the "Anointing Well", and supposedly taking its name from the practice of the ancient druids, and later Christian priests, washing and anointing themselves in its water before undertaking their religious rites. According to tradition, Saint Columba consecrated the site and used water from here to baptise King Brude of the Picts.

The waters of the spring were reputed to act as a cure for cutaneous diseases and in the 19th Century they were widely acclaimed to act against gout and rheumatism. However, it is said that they one day lost their efficacy, when a soldier's wife took her scurvy-stricken child to the location and immersed the infant.

All that can be seen today of Fuaran Allt an Ionnlaid – a dribble of water over stones almost hidden by rank vegetation

In 1650 the Marquis of Montrose, suffering from a fever, drank here on his way to Edinburgh following his capture in Sutherland, watched by crowds of people who had gathered to cheer or jeer his entry to the town. In 1830 the local landowner, H. R. Duff of Muirtown House, enclosed the well in stone and had the topmost stone inscribed with the legend "Luci Fontisque Nymphis" (to the nymphs of the grove and fountain). A paper delivered to the Inverness Scientific Society in 1878 described it thus: "The fountain is pleasantly shaded, beautifully situated, and always affords a cool and refreshing draught." Sadly, that description no longer applies.

The Culloden Wells

Certain parts of Inverness and its surrounds boast a concentration of healing wells, and none more so than Culloden. *Fuaran a' Chlèirich*, the spring of the cleric (also known as *Tobar nan Clèireach,* the well of the clerics) at Balloch (see p. 75) was reputedly a place where religious figures would wash before engaging in rites. *An Tobar Ghorm* (the blue well) was named for the colour of its water and *Tobar na h-Òige* (the well of youth) was reckoned to restore youth to those who washed in, and drank, its water.

Following an ancient practice, Inverness children place cloots on a tree adjacent to Tobar na Coille on the first of May

The most famous was *Tobar na Coille*, the Well of the Wood, also called the Lady Well or St Mary's Well, the last name being accorded to it when this ancient pagan site received a Christian rededication in Catholic times. The pagan practice of visiting this well early on the First of May *(Là Buidhe Bealltainn)*, and hanging a "cloot" to rid oneself of an affliction was only slightly modified by Christian influence, the relevant date becoming the first Sunday of May. Hordes of Invernessians would visit *Tobar na Coille* at this time, a practice that continued until the 1960s. In 1946 over 4,700 people made the trip to the site on special buses. A circular enclosure surrounds the well, with its door facing east; this was once roofed and the place well tended. In 1878, local accountant Alexander Fraser wrote that a woman "... possibly yet alive, acted as a kind of priestess, providing dishes, opening the door of the building which guarded the precincts, and generally kept the place and approach in order." Once situated in a birch wood (hence the name), *Tobar na Coille,* now often called The Culloden Well, is today surrounded by an extensive forestry plantation and can be found at 724452.

Hilton *Baile a' Chnuic*. Little Hiltoun and Mekle Hiltoun are mentioned on the Register of the Great Seal, 1508-9. It

appears likely that the English is a translation of the original Gaelic, although that cannot be certified from the records. A Hugh Maclennan of Hilton was one of W. J. Watson's local place-name informants. A sign on the community centre gives it as *Baile Beag a' Chnuic*, but I have found no historical record of the adjective. *674435*

Holm *An Tolm* in Gaelic, but this name, like **The Haugh**, is probably of English or Scots origin, although the word also existed in Old Norse. Holm can mean "island" but W.J. Watson considered that it here meant "river meadow" which would fit the topography. Watson gave it as *An Tuilm*, but this is most likely its form in the genitive case ("of the Holm") as, according to an 1884 article by Alexander Mackenzie in the journal of The Inverness Scientific Society, the place was known as *Tolm*, while the Laird of Holm was known as *Fear an Tuilm* – the latter demonstrating that the article must also have been used with the nominative form of the name ie *An Tolm*. The Holm Burn is *Allt an Tuilm*. As with "haugh" (talchan), the Gaelic form maintains the pronunciation of the "l" which has been lost in spoken English, although it still exists in the written form. *652421*

Inshes (The) *Na h-Innseagan* The small meadows. Recorded as Inchis in the Inverness Burgh Records, 1556-61. The article is often still heard in connection with the name, a phenomenon which must be a relic of the original Gaelic. Dell of Inshes is *Dail nan Innseagan* (see **Balvonie**). The Inshes Roundabout is at 688445.

Inverness *Inbhir Nis* Mouth of the River Ness. (see **Ness**). The "bh" is pronounced as a "v" in some dialects, and this is why we have Inver, rather than Inner in English (c.f. Innerleithen *(Inbhir Leitheann)* in Peeblesshire). But the records vary between the two, giving variously Invernys (1369 and 1556), Invirnys (1391) and commonly Inner-nes or Innernes in the 16th and 17th Centuries.

Kessock, South *Port Cheasaig* Kessock's port. Given as Kessok in 1437, this ancient crossing point of the Beauly Firth, is reputedly named after the 6th Century saint (also written as Cessog or Kessog) who is intimately associated with Loch Lomond, but who may have had a cell or chapel in this vicinity. Often given in Gaelic as *Port Cheiseig*, the spelling above is more representative of the word's pronunciation. Modern Gaels often refer to South Kessock as *Ceasag a Deas* and **North Kessock** (see below) as *Ceasag a Tuath*. The Kessock Bridge is known in Gaelic as *Drochaid Cheasaig 655472*

Kessock, North *Aiseag Cheasaig* Kessock's ferry (see **South Kessock**). The translated form *Ferry of Kesack* is given on Pont's map of the late 16th Century. *656478*

North Kessock, from Inverness. Before the building of the Kessock Bridge, a ferry plied these waters, both in modern and ancient times.

Kilvean *Cill Bheathain* Church/cell of Saint Bean, an early notable in the Celtic Church, at 662441. Historically the Gaels of Inverness referred to the **Bught** as *Cill Bheathain*, and the Burgh Court Books of 1568 give the "Myln of Kilbean" as an equivalent to the "Mill of Bucht". May's map of 1765 referred to the "arable lands of the Bught, called Keill-a-vean". See **Torvean**. Another local name containing the "kil" element is Kilmuir on the Black Isle (673493). This is *Cille Mhoire* (Mary's cell).

King Duncan's Well *Fuaran Dhonnchaidh* Duncan's well. Popularly thought to refer to King Duncan (killed in battle near Elgin in 1040), but may in fact be named for the Robertson family (*Clann Donnchaidh* in Gaelic) who were at one time Lairds of Culcabock. In a paper to the Inverness Scientific Society and Field Club in 1878, Alexander Fraser gave it as *Furan* [sic] *Lagain Dhonnachaidh* or the Well of King Duncan's Tomb. **King Duncan's grave** is a slight hollow opposite the well on Culcabock Road, which was known in Gaelic as *Clach Dhonnchaidh*

(Duncan's stone i.e. marking his grave) and, in older times, as *Slagan Dhonnchaidh* (Duncan's hollow), an equivalent to the English "King Duncan's Hollow". Historians believe that King Duncan was actually buried on Iona, which would support the hypothesis that connects this site to the Robertsons of Culcabock. *683447*

Kingsmills *Muileann an Rìgh* Mill of the king. Historically a site of several mills using the power of the **Mill Burn**, the rights to which were granted to the townsfolk by royal charter. Two of the six mills along the burn on Pont's map of 1585-95 are given as *Moulyn na Ry (ie Muileann an Rìgh)*. No English equivalent is given on this map. Moll's County Map of Inverness-shire (1725) gives *Mou. Rey*, clearly an abbreviation of the Gaelic. However, an English form is also recorded in the Great Charter of 1591 - Kingsmilns. It is unclear as to whether the area was referred to in the singular or plural in Gaelic (ie *Muileann an Rìgh* or *Muilnean an Rìgh*). In John Thomson's Atlas of Scotland (1832), only one mill is shown and the name is singular – Kingsmill. *676445*

Kinmylies *Ceann a' Mhìlidh* Warrior's headland. The name is very old, appearing in Alexander II's charter of 1232 which granted the land of "Kinmyly" to the Bishop of Moray. It appears as Kinmylis in the Inverness Burgh Records of 1556-61. W.J Watson compared it to Carmylie in Fife. *645447*

Knocknagael Commonly given as *Cnoc nan Giall*, hill of the hostages. Older recorded forms are Knokyngill, Knokyngeile and Knokingall. If the interpretation is correct, the locality may have been named after an agreement was reached on the hill which included the giving of hostages as surety. *659408*

Leachkin (The) *An Leacainn* The broad slope/hillside. The word is commonly *leacann* but in Inverness it appears in its slenderised dative form. Gaelic-speakers pronounce the word in English as it is in Gaelic, but some English-speakers pronounce it "Larkin". The origin of the name, however, is indisputable. It fits perfectly the location, on the slopes west of the Ness between Craig Phadrig and Kinmylies (see opposite). *636445*

The aptly named slopes of The Leachkin (An Leacainn) as viewed from the River Ness. The community here was still strongly Gaelic in character in the late 19th Century

Leys (The) *An Leigheas* The meaning is uncertain. A 19th Century Gaelic poem to William Mackenzie, the "Leys Bard", who taught there for forty years, referred to "iomadh bliadhna san Leidheas" (many years in The Leys), demonstrating the presence of the article and the word's pronunciation but leaving us no wiser as to its meaning. Watson gave *An Leigheas* (meaning unknown). The oldest record is as The Leys in the Inverness Burgh Records of 1556-61, but it appears with two syllables (Leyis), as in the Gaelic, on a map dating from ca. 1600. A number of commentators have suggested *An Lèas* - the bright (i.e. sunny) place, but this is cannot be accepted with certainty. The Oldtown of Leys (668412) is *Seanabhaile an Leigheis* and Leys Castle (680410) is *Caisteal an Leigheis.*

Lochardil *Loch Àrdail* Reputedly the name of an old barony. The meaning of *àrdail* is obscure. When the Ordnance Survey did its work in 1868-70, it was merely the name of a field on the Drummond Estate of Charles Fraser-Mackintosh, the loch having been filled in long before. The owner, who was a local informant for the Ordnance Survey, insisted the name be preserved on the map as he intended to build a house there! The dwelling is now a hotel, situated at 662428, and Lochardil is now the name of the surrounding suburb.

Lochgorm *An Loch Gorm* The green loch. An old inlet of the Moray Firth which extended into the vicinity of the current Safeway supermarket on Millburn Rd. It became isolated from the main body of the firth, grew stagnant and was filled in during the 19th Century. John Fraser in his *Reminiscences of Inverness (1905)* reports that it still existed in the 1840s (giving its name to the nearby Lochgorm Inn), and the area between the Crown and the road leading to Ardersier is

given as *Loch Gorm* in a map of the town drawn up to show parliamentary boundaries in 1832, although no obvious water body is delineated. The name today would be almost forgotten except that it is perpetuated in a local furniture business which stands adjacent to the site of the ancient loch.

Loch na Sanais *Loch na Seanais* Watson gave it as a derivative of *Loch na Sean-innse,* meaning loch of the old meadow or haugh. Unfortunately a mistake made by the Ordnance Survey gave it as Loch na Sanais which ostensibly means "Loch of the Whisper", an appellation which is explained by a delightful, if apocryphal, story of young love (see p 84). *Sanas* is generally a masculine word, so that *Loch an t-Sanais* would be the expected form; however it may be that it was feminine in the local dialect, since a stone near Croy is called *Clach na Sanais* in Gaelic and The Whispering Stone in English (it reputedly commemorates a whispered warning of treachery during a feud between the Cummings and Mackintoshes). But this is made irrelevant by the pronunciation of the Inverness name which is "Loch na Shanish" not "Loch na Sanish". This was explained to the OS by three separate informants in the 1860s, but the surveyors preferred the single opinion of Charles Fraser-Mackintosh who unfortunately ascribed to the "whisper" hypothesis. The loch is to be found on the Torvean Golf Course at 652437.

Longman (The) Probably the most enigmatic place name in Inverness. Its origin is unknown and the Gaelic today is either just as the English i.e. *An Longman* (always with the article), or the descriptive *An Raon Rèidh* ("the level plain"), a name coined in the 20th Century. A Gaelic origin for *Longman* has been suggested – "Ship flat", derived from *long* (ship) and *mìn* (flat), but this is almost certainly a falsehood. Folk etymology has also been at work, creating a story of a "long man" whose drowned body was washed ashore and then buried in this area (at what was called Longman's Grave and marked as such on Home's 1774 map), and yet another of the receivers of contraband goods elevating a figure of a "long man" on a pole as a sign to smugglers to land their wares. Again, these are hardly credible. If its origins are Gaelic, the

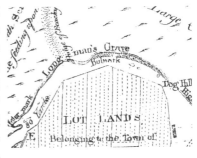

terminal "an" might represent a diminutive, rather than a plural (for example, *lochan* can mean both "lochs" and "small loch"), as the article, at least in modern Gaelic, is a singular one. However, the name is recorded in a Gaelic story told by Donnchadh Mac a' Bheathain of Croachy in Strath Nairn, reproduced in the Transactions of the Gaelic Society of Inverness (Vol XLVII). In it he said *chon na Longmans* (to the Longman). The preposition *chon (chun)* takes the genitive case which means that Longman is here either a singular feminine noun or, perhaps more likely, a plural noun. The terminal "s", after the English fashion, suggests that the (presumably bilingual) speaker considered it to be grammatically plural, although it might also indicate that

Loch na Sanais

Folk etymology has been at work as much in Inverness as in other places, and it is responsible for a pleasant local story which "explains" how the loch got its supposed name "Loch of the Whisper". As is explained on p. 82-83, this derivation of the name is nonsense, as the loch is properly *Loch na Seanais* (loch of the old meadow) – but that shouldn't stop us telling the story…

There was a beautiful girl, the daughter of a smith, who lived at Kilvean near Torvean. Her father wanted her to marry a rich merchant in Inverness but she had other ideas, for she fancied a fine looking young man from Dochfour, even though he was almost penniless. The smith and the merchant decided to give the lad a beating so that he would not come near the daughter again.

The merchant and a companion in crime ambushed the boyfriend in Coille nam Bodach, close to the loch, which was then unnamed or perhaps went by a different name. But the lad was too tough by far and he sent the assailants packing with broken teeth and black eyes. The smith was furious when he heard what had happened.

Some short time afterwards, the girl was taking a walk close to the loch when she noticed two men coming towards her. They, however, had not noticed her. She recognised them – it was her father and the merchant – and she leapt behind a bush, where she remained in hiding.

As the men walked past her, they were talking in a whisper *("ann an sanas")*, saying to each other that the only solution to the problem was to murder the young man. After they had gone, instead of returning home, the lass went hurriedly to Dochfour, to her boyfriend's house, to warn him of the plan. They eloped together and were married within a month. When the people of the area heard what had happened, and that the murder had been avoided by the girl hearing the terrible plan in a whisper, they called the loch "Loch na Sanais" – loch of the whisper.

the word is not originally Gaelic or, if it is, that its origins had become entirely opaque to Gaels of the modern era. The "long" might be a corruption of *lann* (enclosure, house, often associated with a religious establishment), although there is no Inverness tradition to support that, or perhaps of *lòn* (meadow, pond, tidal pool) – as this area would have been a mass of rough tidal flats in medieval times. The Kessock Bridge meets the Longman at *669473.*

Merkinch *Marc-Innis* Horse-island or horse-meadow.  The word *marc,* no longer a standard word for "horse" is preserved in *marcachd,* the Gaelic for "riding". Given as Markhynch in 1365 and as both Merkinsh and Markinsh in the Wardlaw Manuscript, the universal pronunciation of the name as "MERK-insh" rather than "MARK-insh" is by no means ancient. Local lads are reported as referring to themselves in English as "MARK-nish boys", after the Gaelic fashion, in the 19th Century, and the English spoken here was for long peppered with Gaelic loan-words such as spatchel (*spaideal,* smart), and greeshag (*greiseag,* a short spell). This flat land was once an island in the Ness delta, used as a common-grazing for horses (see **Capel Inch**). *658462*

Mill Burn *Allt a' Mhuilinn* Burn of the mill. Pont's map of the late 16th Century gives it as *Alt Moulyn nen Ry,* without any English equivalent. This is *Allt Muileann an Rìgh* (literally, Burn of the King's Mill), for the power of this burn was used to drive the mills whose site was granted to the townsfolk by royal charter. (See **Kingsmills**). The modern name for the burn (as opposed to the site of the mills) no longer carries a monarchical reference in either language. Millburn Academy (at 676455) is *Acadamaidh Allt a' Mhuilinn* in Gaelic.

Milton *Baile a' Mhuilinn* Mill town. A common place name, found in several locations around Inverness, and meaning a settlement where a mill existed, powered by the water of a burn. The closest to the city centre is the Milton sandwiched between Hilton and Culcabock at 677439. The settlement no longer exists as a discrete entity, but the area close to the Mill Burn in this vicinity is still referred to as Milton *(Baile a' Mhuilinn),* and the name is perpetuated in Milton Crescent. Another example is Milton of Leys *(Baile Muilinn an Leigheis).*

Moray Firth Generally *Linne Mhoireibh* in Gaelic today. Moireabh/Moray is an ancient name of Celtic origin probably meaning "sea settlement". Other Gaelic forms are An Linne Mhoireach and An Geob Moireach.

Muckovie *Mucamhaigh* Pig field or pig plain. An ancient name, according to W.J. Watson. Lower Muckovie is at 705434

Muirtown *Baile an Fhraoich* Township of the heather (moor). Given as Moortoun in the Wardlaw Manuscript of the late 17th Century, the English is a translation of the Gaelic, according to a 1917 paper of the Inverness Scientific Society. *650460*

Ness, River *Abhainn Nis* The river is given as *Nesa* in the (Latin) *Life of Columba* by Adamnan. Nesa is thought to have been a river goddess worshipped by the ancients. The English *Ness* represents the old Gaelic nominative form which no longer exists in that language. What we have today in the Gaelic *Nis* is the genitive form (i.e. "of the Ness"), as in *Inbhir Nis* (Inverness). Loch Ness *(Loch Nis)* was named after the river. The Ness Islands were long known to locals by their Gaelic appellation *(Na h-Eileanan)*, as is demonstrated by the Inverness Burgh Records of the mid to late 16th Century which record them as Ellon, Ellan and Ellanis.

Ord Hill *An t-Òrd, Cnoc an Ùird.* The English is tautological as is the Gaelic *Cnoc an Ùird*, as *òrd* means a steep rounded hill, a perfect description of this eminence which overlooks the north end of Kessock Bridge. *664491*

Raigmore *An Ràthaig Mhòr* The large fortified dwelling. *Ràthaig* is a derivative of the commoner word *ràth*. The name is Gaelic but not indigenous to Inverness. It arrived with the building of Raigmore House by Mackintosh of Raigmore (in Strathdearn) in the 19th century, and it came to be applied to an area previously called The Machrie (the plain) and which was also named Broomtown in the 19th Century. Raigmore Hospital (at 687447) is called in Gaelic (somewhat ungrammatically) *Ospadal an Ràthaig Mhòir*.

Resaurie *An Ruigh Samhraidh* The summer pasture. A place where cattle would be grazed in summer. *706451*

Ruighard *An Ruigh Àrd* The high slope. *Ruigh* is a difficult word to translate into

English. In this instance it probably refers to the outstretched gentle slope running to the north-east of Dunain Hill. *634436*

Scorguie *An Sgòr Gaoithe* The windy point. Given as Scorguy on Home's map of 1774. *645463*

Scretan Burn *Allt an Sgrìodain* Burn of the stony ravine. This stream, descriptively named but now much altered, flows through what was part of the old "Lands of Drakie" between The Inshes and the Moray Firth. *697453*

Slackbuie *An Slag Buidhe* The yellow hollow. Most likely named for the masses of yellow buttercups which grow there in summer (where the ground is not now covered by houses). Upper Slackbuie was formerly known as "Knocknakirk" *(Cnoc na Circe)*, the hill of the hen, possibly meaning grouse. *672422*

Smithton *Baile a' Ghobhainn* Blacksmith's steading/township. *713453*

Stoneyfield Bòrd na Gàidhlig has given the name *Fèith nan Clach* to this area in the east of the city, now the site of their headquarters. This is the Gaelic given by Watson for Stoneyfield in Easter Ross. The only Gaelic form I have found for the Inverness example is given by John Noble (1891) as "...Stoneyfield, or - a name it was better known by among Invernessians in those early days - Scrìodan-sgràd..." The first element is Sgrìodan for the burn (see Scretan above) but the second remains cryptic.

Tobar na h-Òige see **Culloden Wells** p. 77.

Tomnahurich *Tom na h-Iùbhraich* Hill of the yew wood. Given as Tomahury on Roy's military map of 1747-55 and Tomnahurach by John Home in 1774, this name has been the subject of much discussion over the years, perhaps stemming from the three different forms given in the Wardlaw Manuscript: Tom ni Fyrich, Tomnifirish and Tomnihurich. The modern Gaelic interpretation is now generally accepted as being faithful to the original although, writing in the Transactions of the Gaelic Society of Inverness in 1925, Roderick Barron claimed that its local pronunciation as *Tom na Chiùraich*, allied to oral reports of the Gaelic-speaking people of Glenurquhart calling it *Tom na fyrich* as late as the 1850s, suggested that there had once been an initial "f" in the second element (perhaps relating to *fiodh, fiodhrach*, wood or timber). The hill, now a cemetery, has a special place in the cultural history of Inverness, being reputedly an abode of the fairies and the subject of many a spooky tale in Gaelic and English. *655442*

Torbreck *An Tòrr Breac* The speckled hill. A settlement just to the south of the city. *649409*

Torvean *Tòrr Bheathain* Hill of Saint Bean. The spelling on Home's (1774) map – Torevain Hill – gives a better idea of the pronunciation than does the modern rendering. According to tradition the saint was a cousin of Columba, and built a religious cell in the vicinity of the hill (see **Kilvean**). If that is true, the name is very old indeed. The Old Statistical Account of 1793 tells of a "very large cairn near the river" at the foot of Torvean, which was presumably removed during the building of the Caledonian Canal, and in which a "coffin was found composed of six thick flags. This is supposed to be the dormitory of Bean, a saint of the Culdee order, from whom the place and hill derive their names". *648433*

Torvean is the hill at left, viewed across the Bught Park, with Tomnahurich on the right. This park is one of Scotland's major locations for the playing of shinty, the ancient sport of the Gael.

Mar a Fhuair Loch Nis ainm

What follows is a traditional story which tells how Loch Ness got its name (and which should be taken with a generous grain of salt). As it is a play on words, it makes little sense in translation...

Ochionn fhad an t-saoghail bha an Gleann Mòr, a tha a-nis fo uisgeachan domhainn Loch Nis, tioram ach a-mhàin gu robh abhainn bheag chiùin a' sruthadh troimhe gu mall. Bha bonn a' ghlinne anabarrach brèagha, le iomadh seòrsa de dh'fheur is lus beag. Air gach taobh dheth, bha beanntan àrda an ìre mhath còmhdaichte le coilltean àlainn. Bha daoine gu math pailt anns a' ghleann ach, a dh'aindeoin sin, cha robh dad a dhìth orra.

Air bruach na h-aibhne, bha tobar ann a bha le draoidh air an robh Dàlaidh Mòr mar ainm. Bha an t-uisge ann glan is soilleir, agus dhèanadh e leigheas air gach tinneas a bh' air muinntir an àite. Bha e ceadaichte do dhuine sam bith a thogradh uisge a tharraing às.

Aig beul an tobair bha clach agus thug an draoidh seachad rabhadh don t-sluagh – cho luath 's a bhiodh duine deiseil às dèidh dha an t-uisge a tharraing, dh'fheumadh e a' chlach a chur air ais na h-àite fhèin. Mura tachradh sin, thuirt e, chuireadh am fuaran an tìr fo sgrios.

Chreideadh an sluagh na thuirt Dàlaidh riutha agus bha e na chleachdadh aca uile a' chlach a chur air ais air beul an tobair gach turas a tharraingeadh iad uisge às. Chaidh na làithean is na bliadhnaichean seachad, agus muinntir a' ghlinne uile ann an deagh shunnd.

Là de na làithean, dh'fhàg bean òg a leanabh anns an taigh agus dh'fhalbh i a dh'iarraidh uisge às an tobar. Thog i a' chlach far an tobair agus chuir i air an dàrna taobh i. Ach dìreach nuair a bha i a' dol a thogail uisge, chuala i glaodh bhon taigh a dh'innis dhi gu robh a leanabh faisg air an teine agus ann an cunnart. Rinn i air an taigh na deann agus shàbhail i a leanabh. Ach dhìochuimhnich i na thuirt Dàlaidh Mòr agus cha do chuir i a' chlach air ais air ceann an tobair mar bu chòir.

Thòisich an t-uisge air èirigh agus an ceann ùine glè ghoirid bha e a' brùchdadh a-mach às an tobar. Mus deach aire an t-sluaigh a tharraing gu na thachair, bha an tobar air chall ann am meadhan locha. Cha b' fhada gus an robh an gleann air fad còmhdaichte le uisge.

Rinn muinntir a' ghlinne air na beanntan airson a bhith sàbhailte os cionn na tuile. Bha iad a' caoineadh is a' caoidh gu goirt mu chall an dachaighean, agus cha robh ach aona ghlaodh ri chluinntinn air feadh na sgìre: "Tha loch a-nis ann! Tha loch a-nis ann!"

Agus 's ann bhuaithe sin a fhuair na h-uisgeachan ùra an t-ainm "Loch Nis", ainm a th' againn fhathast an-diugh.

Buidheachas

Sincere thanks are due to the following organisations for their assistance:

HI~ARTS

Inverness & Nairn
ENTERPRISE

COMUNN NA GÀIDHLIG

am baile THE GAELIC VILLAGE

Highland History and Culture
www.ambaile.org.uk

The Gaelic Society of Inverness *(Comunn Gàidhlig Inbhir Nis)* was established in 1871 for the purpose of "cultivating the language, poetry and music of the Scottish Highlands and generally furthering the interests of the Gaelic-speaking people". More information is available at www.gsi.org.uk.

'S e **Fòram Gàidhlig Inbhir Nis** buidheann coimhearsnachd a tha ag amas air piseach a thoirt air suidheachadh na Gàidhlig ann an Inbhir Nis. Gheibhear tuilleadh fiosrachaidh aig www.inbhirnis.org.

Fòram Gàidhlig Inbhir Nis
Guth na Coimhearsnachd
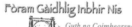

Thanks go to all those historians and place name scholars upon whose researches I have drawn heavily. I am much obliged also to the staff of the Reference section of Inverness Library and Highland Council Archives, and to Murdo MacLeod, Honorary Librarian of the Gaelic Society of Inverness. Special thanks go to Peadar Morgan for advice on place names, and to Brian Ó hEadhra, John Storey and Allan MacLeod for their encouragement, assistance and advice. Taing mhòr do Chearaidh cuideachd, airson mo bhrosnachadh. Any mistakes are entirely my own.

Note on illustrations: The photographs on pp 10, 14, 53, 55 and 66 come from the archives of Am Baile (see top of this page). Unless otherwise indicated, all map details come from Home's map of Inverness (1774)

90

Bibliography

Alexander, Fraser *Ancient Wells in the North and their Folklore* Transactions of the Inverness Scientific Society and Field Club Vol. 1 1875-80, p. 119-146.

Anderson, A. O. and M. O., *Adomnan's Life of Columba.* Edinburgh 1961.

Anderson, I.H. *Inverness before Railways.* 1885.

Barron, Evan *Inverness in the Fifteenth Century* R. Carruthers & Sons, Inverness 1906.

Barron, Evan *Inverness in the Middle Ages* Transactions of the Inverness Scientific Society and Field Club Vol. 7. 1906-12 p. 33-65.

Barron, Evan MacLeod *Inverness and the MacDonalds.* Robert Carruthers & Sons, Inverness, 1930.

Barron, Hugh *Notes on Bards.* Transactions of the Gaelic Society of Inverness Vol XLVIII 1972-4 p. 1-13

Barron, Roderick *Dorlach Fhacal.* Transactions of the Gaelic Society of Inverness Vol XLII 1925 p. 1-5

Burt, Edmund *Letters from a Gentleman in the North of Scotland.* London 1754; reprinted 1998.

Cameron, George *A History and Description of the Town of Inverness.* 1847.

Celtic Magazine, The *Various unattributed papers.* Alexander MacKenzie, High St., Inverness.

Durkacz, Victor Edward *The Decline of the Celtic Languages.* John Donald, Edinburgh 1983.

Dwelly, Edward *The Illustrated Gaelic-English Dictionary.* 1901-11. Republished Birlinn, Edinburgh 1993.

Dwelly, Edward (compiler), **Clyne, Douglas** (ed.) and **Thomson, Derick** *Appendix to Dwelly's Gaelic-English Dictionary.* Gairm, Glasgow, 1991.

Fraser, John *Reminiscences of Inverness.* 1905.

Fraser-Mackintosh, Charles *Invernessiana: a history of the town and parish of Inverness from 1160 to 1599.* Inverness, 1875.

Fraser-Mackintosh, Charles *The Lower Fishings of the Ness* Celtic Magazine Vol 8.

Garnett, T. *Observations on a tour through the Highlands Vol 2* John Stockdale, London 1811.

Hall, Rev. James *Travels in Scotland* London 1807.

Home, John *map of Inverness, 1774. Copy held by Highland Council Archives, Inverness.*

Inverness Burgh Records 1556-1561 *(transcribed 1899), held in Highland Council Archives, Inverness.*

Inverness Field Club *Loch Ness and Thereabouts.* Inverness, 1991.

Inverness Field Club *The Hub of the Highlands: the book of Inverness and District.* Inverness, 1990.

Joyce, P.W. *The Origin and History of Irish Names of Places.* Dublin 1883.

Longmore, Leonella *Inverness in the 18th Century.* 2001

Mac Bheathain, Alasdair *Dain agus Orain Ghàidhlig le Màiri Nic a'Phearsain (Màiri nighean Iain Bhàin).* A & U MacCoinnich, Inbhir Nis 1891.

Macbain, Alexander *Personal names and surnames of the town of Inverness* Inverness 1895

Macbain, Alexander *Place Names of Inverness-shire* Transactions of the Gaelic Society of Inverness Vol XXV 1902 p. 55-83.

Macbain, Alexander *Place Names of the Highlands and Islands of Scotland.* Eneas MacKay, Stirling 1922.

MacBheathean, Seumas *Danaibh Spioradail agus Marbh-rainn air Dhiadhairibh Urramach* Inbhir Nis 1880.

MacChoinnich, Iain *Eachdraidh a' Phrionnsa no Bliadhna Thearlaich.* Dùn Eideann 1844.

MacDonald, Rev. A *The MacDonald Collection of Gaelic Poetry* Inverness 1911.

MacDougall, Rev. James & Rev. George Calder (ed) *Folk Tales and Fairy Lore.* John Grant, Edinburgh 1910

MacIlleathain, Ruairidh *Seachd Sgeulachdan às Inbhir Nis* Clàr, Inbhir Nis 1998.

MacIntosh, Murdoch *A History of Inverness.* Highland News Ltd, Inverness, 1939.

Mackay, W & C. Boyd (eds) *Records of Inverness. Vol. 1 (Burgh Court Books 1556-86)* and *Vol. 2 (Burgh Court Books 1602-37 & Minutes of Town Council 1637-88).* New Spalding Club, Aberdeen 1911.

MacKay, William *The Celtic Element in Old Inverness.* Trans. Gaelic Soc. Inverness, Vol 28, p 224-237. 1914.

MacKay, William (ed.) *Wardlaw Manuscript compiled by Rev. James Fraser ca. 1666-1700.*

MacKenzie, Alexander *Local Topography* Transactions of the Gaelic Society of Inverness Vol. I 1872 p. 23-31.

MacKenzie, Alexander *The Gaelic origins of local names* Transactions of the Inverness Scientific Society and Field Club Vol. 3 1883-8 p. 9-17.

MacKenzie, John *The Beauties of Gaelic Poetry (Sàr Obair nam Bàrd Gaelach)* John Grant, Edinburgh 1907.

Maclean, John *Reminiscences of a Clachnacuddin Nonagenarian.* Donald MacDonald, Inverness, 1886.

Meek, Donald *Mairi Mhòr nan Oran.* Gairm, Glaschu, 1977.

Meldrum, Edward *From Nairn to Loch Ness. Local History and Archaeology Guidebook No. 1.* Inverness, 1983.

Meldrum, Edward *From Loch Ness to the Aird. Local History and Archaeology Guidebook No. 2.* Inverness, 1987.

Meldrum, Edward *Inverness. Local History and Archaeology Guidebook No. 4.* Inverness, 1982.

Meldrum, Edward *Private notes held by Highland Council Archives, Inverness.*

Morris, Ruth & Frank *Scottish Healing Wells* Alethea Press, Sandy 1982.

National Library of Scotland *various historic maps and documents available on their internet site (free of charge) at* www.nls.uk.

Newton, Norman *The Life and Times of Inverness.* John Donald, Edinburgh 1996.

Noble, John *Miscellanea Invernessiana.* Eneas MacKay, Stirling, 1902.

Noble, John *The Witch of Inverness and the Fairies of Tomnahurich* Inverness 1891.

Ordnance Survey *Name Books and old maps held in Highland Council Archives, Inverness.*

Pollitt, Gerald A. *Historic Inverness.* The Melven Press, Perth, 1981.

Rose, J (ed.) *Metrical Reliques of "The Men" in the Highlands* Inverness 1851

Ross, Alexander *Old Inverness* Transactions of the Inverness Scientific Society and Field Club Vol. 2 1881-3 p. 64-92.

Ross, Alexander *Some More Notes on Old Inverness* Transactions of the Inverness Scientific Society and Field Club Vol. 8 1912-18 p. 283-302

Sinclair, Rev. John *The Black Isle* The Celtic Monthly. Inverness 1898.

Short Account of the Town of Inverness Edinburgh 1828

The First Statistical Account of Scotland Vol 9. 1793.

The Statistical Account of Inverness-Shire William Blackwood & Sons, Edinburgh 1842.

Transactions of the Inverness Scientific Society and Field Club *Various unattributed papers.*

Wallace, Thomas *Notes on the Early Churches* Transactions of the Inverness Scientific Society and Field Club Vol. 2 1881-3 p. 64-92.

Watson, William J. *The history of the Celtic place-names of Scotland* William Blackwood & Sons Ltd., Edinburgh 1926.

Watson, William J. *Prints of the Past: around Inverness.* Inverness 1909.

Watson, William J. *Scottish Place-Name Papers.* Steve Savage, London 2002.

Withers, Charles W. J. *Gaelic in Scotland 1698-1981: the geographical history of a language.* John Donald, Edinburgh, 1984.

Withers, Charles W. J. *Gaelic Scotland: the transformation of a culture region* Routledge, London and New York, 1988.

Index

Abban, The 56, 62
Abriachan 33
Ach-na-boddich 46
Adamnan 15
Aldnacreich 45
Allanfearn 57
Allt a' Mhuilinn 85
Allt an Sgrìodain 53, 87
Allt Muineach An t- 21, 46, 75
Allt na Banaraich 45
Allt na Caillich 45
Allt na Crìche 45
Allt na h-Imire 45
Allt nan Sgitheach 58
Allt Shiamaidh 45
Alturlie 57
Anointing Well see Fuaran Allt an Ionnlaid
Archie Bui 33
Ardersier 71
Ashie, Loch 74
Auldinhemmerie 45
Aultmuniack see Allt Muineach
Aultnaskiach see Allt nan Sgitheach

Baile a' Chnuic 59, 78
Baile a' Ghobhainn 87
Baile a' Mhonaidh 60
Baile a' Mhuilinn 59
Baile an Fhraoich 59
Baile an Loch 58
Baile an Lòin 58
Baile Lachlainn 46
Baile Mhic Phàdraig 28, 46
Baile na Coille 60
Baile na Creige 59, 69
Baile na Faire 58
Baile na Gàig 59
Baile na h-Èileig 47
Baile nam Bodach 46
Baile nam Feadag 59
Baile place names 59
Baile Raibeirt 60
Baile Theàrlaich 64
Baillie, Maria 26
Baillie, Rev. Robert 22
Ballifeary 17, 58

Balloan 28, 58
Balloch 58
Balloch, The 46
Balmore of Leys 59
Bal-na-boddich 46
Balnacraig 59
Balnafare 17
Balnafettack 59
Balnagaig 59
Balnahairn 46
Balnakyle 60
Balphadrig 28, 60
Balrobert 60
Balvonie of Inshes 47, 60
Bealach, Am 46
Bean, Saint 79, 88
Beaton, Colin 26
Beauly 60
Beauly Firth 60
Bell's School 35
Bellachlan 46
Bellahellich 47
Black Isle 60
Bogbain 60-61
Boyd, H. C. 11
Brayrinchaltin 47
Brecknish 57
Broichan 16
Brude, King 16, 76
Bruichmor-caltine 47
Bught, Mill of 79
Bught, The 61, 79, 88
Burt, Edmund 24

Cabog Day 28
Caiplich, The 47, 48
Cairnlaw 46, 62
Caisteal na Lethoir 26, 63
Caisteal Rollach 62
Caisteal St̀ll 64
Caledonian Canal 62
Cameron, Samuel 33
Capall Innis 6, 48, 62
Capel Inch 6, 48, 62
Càrn an Fhuarain 47, 49
Càrn Dubh, An 63

Carnarc Point 6, 62-63
Carneinwarrane 47, 49
Carse, The 63
Castlc Hcather 26, 63
Castle Hill 64
Castle Leathers 63
Castlehill (Auld/MacBeth's) 69
Castlehill (of Inshes) 64
Cauldeen 64
Censuses 39, 40-41
Central Primary School 42, 43
Chapel Yard 35, 64
Charleston/Charlestown 64
Chars, A' 63
Cherry, The 6, 64
Cholera 75
Churrie Dyke 65
Cill Bheathain 17, 61, 79
Clach na Cùdainn 4, 13, 31, 66
Clach na Sanais 83
Clachan Donachy 48
Clachnacuddin see Clach na Cùdainn
Clachnacuddin Nonagenarian see Maclean, John
Clachnagaick see Clachnahagaig
Clachnahagaig 67
Clachnaharry 25, 38, 42, 51, 68
Cladh Mòr, An 64
Clann Mhic an t-Sasannaich 26
Cnoc a' Ghaorra 25, 49
Cnoc an Tionail 49
Cnoc Dubh, An 49
Cnoc na Circe 49, 87
Cnoc na Crìche 49
Cnoc nan Gad 50
Cnoc nan Gobhar 48
Coille nam Bodach 84
Columba, Saint 15, 16, 76
Cradlehall 68
Craig Dunain 48, 74
Craig Phadrig see Creag Phàdraig
Craigton 69
Crannog 62-63
Crèadh Innis 48
Creag Dhùn Eun 74
Creag Phàdraig 68-69, 81
Creibh Mhòr 21
Cromwell, Oliver 12, 24, 25-26, 49
Crown, The 15, 69, 82
Cùil Daothail 69
Cùil in place names 70
Cùil Lodair 70

Cùil na Càbaig 69
Culcabock 46, 54, 69, 85
Culclachie 48
Culduthel 69
Cullernie 70
Culloden 26, 70, 74
Cumming, Jocky 34
Cuthbert, George 21

Dail an Eich 6, 48, 71
Dàlaidh Mòr 89
Dalcross 27, 71
Dalneigh 6, 48, 71-72
Dalreoch 72
Daviot 72
Dealganros 27, 71
Defoe, Daniel 12
Deimhidh 72
Dennis, Doda 43
Dhùghallach, Seònaid 26
Diriebught 72
Dochfour 72, 84
Dochgarroch 72
Dochnacraig 72-73
Doire nam Bochd 72
Dòmhnall Sgoilear 33
Dòmhnallach, Am Bàrd 26
Dores 72
Drakies 73
Druim Aithisidh 6
Druim Buidhe see Drumbuie
Druim Dìomhain see Drumdevan
Drumbuie 71, 74
Drumdevan 74
Drummond 74
Drumossie 6, 74
Duff family 38, 76
Dùn Eun 74
Dunain 54, 59, 72, 74

Essich 75

Fairies 31, 32
Feabuie 58
Fear an Tuilm 78
Fèith nan Clach 87
Finlay Dhu 28
Fionn MacCumhail 31
Fluke Inn 46, 75
Fraser, Alexander 77
Fraser, Colonel James 27, 69

Fraser, David 21
Fraser, John 28, 29, 55, 82
Fraser-Mackintosh, Charles 30, 40, 82, 83
Fuaran a' Chladaich 75
Fuaran a' Chlèirich 75
Fuaran a' Chragain Bhric 48
Fuaran a' Mhaighstir 49
Fuaran Allt an Ionnlaid 75, 76
Fuaran Dearg, Am 48
Fuaran Dhonnchaidh 80
Fuaran na Ceapaich 49
Fuaran na Làire Bàine 49
Fuaran na Priseig 51

Gaelic in the Courts 38-39
Gaelic in Education 38, 40, 43
Gaelic in the Churches 34-37
Gaelic Society of Inverness 19, 39-40, 88
Gaelic stories from Inverness 31, 32, 89
Gaelic words in Inverness English 20, 85
Garnett, Thomas 25
Glas Chàrn na Crìche 49
Glascarnenacreich see Glas Chàrn na Crìche
Glebe, The 50
Glìob, An see Glebe, The
Graidhe an Uisge 48, 49

Hall, Rev. James 29
Haugh, The 73, 75
High Church 35
Highland Council 42
Hilton 59, 78, 85
Holm 73, 78
Home, John 58, 59, 83
Horses 10, 48, 62, 85

Inglis, Provost 72
Innseagan, Na h- see Inshes
Inshes (The) 78
Inverness Royal Academy 44
Inverness Society for the Support of Gaelic
    Schools 38

Jock on the Maggot 50, 67
Johnson, Samuel 12

Kessock Bridge 52, 69, 85
Kessock Ferry 14, 79
Kessock, North & South 79
Kessock, Saint 51
Kilmuir 79

Kilvean 17, 79, 84
King Duncan's Grave 54, 80
King Duncan's Hollow 54, 80
King Duncan's Well 80
Kingsmills 80, 85
Kinmylies 28, 46, 60, 80
Kirk, Thomas 12, 20
Knockdow 49
Knockgur 25, 49
Knockintinnel 49
Knocknacreich 47, 49
Knocknagad 50
Knocknagael 81
Knocknakirk 49, 87

Lag a' Challtainn see Lagchaltin
Lagchaltin 50
Làrach an Taigh Mhòir 69
Leachkin, The 28, 81
Leigheas, An 81
Leys 28, 49, 81-82, 85
Loch na Sanais 82-83, 84
Loch Nis 89
Lochardil 60, 82
Lochgorm 82
Longman 83, 85

MacBhàtair Uilleam see Watson, William J
Mac Iain Ruaidh 33
Macaulay, Lord 11, 42
Macbain, Alexander 40
MacBeth (King) 15
MacDonald, Kenneth 11
MacDonald, Thomas 26
MacDougall, Janet 26
Machrie, The 50, 86
MacIntosh, Murdoch 67
Mackay, John 12, 23-24
Mackay, William 19
Mackenzie, Alexander 71, 78
Mackenzie, Kenneth 26
Mackenzie, Rev. Hector 22
Mackenzie, William 28, 46, 49, 81
Mackintosh, Lachlan 75
MacLachlan, Lachlan 26
Maclean, John 21, 33, 35, 36, 66-67, 75
MacLeod, Hugh 39
MacOldonich, Alexander 26
MacPherson, Mary see Màiri Mhòr nan Òran
Maggot, The 50
Màiri Mhòr nan Òran 30-31, 74

Marc Innis 6, 48
McCulloch, Rev. Duncan 22
McKay, Anne 24
Merkinch 6, 41, 42, 48, 62, 85
Millburn 21, 45, 46, 80, 85
Millburn Academy 72, 85
Milton 59, 85
Ministear na Feusaig 37
Monster, River Ness 16
Montrose, Marquis of 76
Moray Firth 86
Morrison, Rev. 37
Muckovie 47, 49, 54, 74, 86
Muileann an Rìgh 80
Muirtown 25, 26, 75, 76

Nairnside 48
Names, feminine forms 18-19
Names, personal 17-20
Ness Islands 86
Ness, Loch 16
Ness, River 16, 33, 51, 52, 56-57, 62, 66-67, 86
Nicknames 19, 28-29
Norse place names 52, 73

Ord Hill 86

Patronymics 18-20
Petty 73
Pictish place names 72, 73
Picts 15, 16
Poll an Ròid 60
Poll Crèadha, Am 51
Poll Cruaidh, Am 54
Polla Criadh see Poll Crèadha, Am
Pollitt, Gerald 12
Polvanie 51
Pont, Timothy 79, 80
Priseag Well 49, 51
Pusag 51

Raigmore 86
Raining's School 38
Resaurie 86
Robertsons of Culcabock 54, 80
Ronach 49
Rose Street 52
Ross, Alexander 57, 62
Ross, James 22
Ruigh Samhraidh, An 86
Ruighard 86

Sabhal Daraich, An 31
Scalp na Caorach 49
Scalp Phàdraig Mhòir 49
Scalps 49
Scatgate 52
Scorguie 54, 87
Scots names 61, 73, 75, 78
Scretan Burn 53, 87
Scriodan-sgràd 53
Second sight 36-37
Sgòr Gaoithe 87
Shinty 61, 88
Shirra Dhu 33
Shoes, Gaelic names 33
Slackbuie 87
Slacknamarlach see Slag nam Mèirleach
Slag Buidhe, An 87
Slag nam Mèirleach 54
Slochd Dunache 54
Smithton 87
Sràid na Croiche 52
St. Mary's Well 77
Stac an Fhithich 54
Stewart, John Roy 70-71
Stoneyfield 53, 87
Stuart, Rev. William 23

Talchan, An 75
Tobar Ghorm, An 77
Tobar na Coille 77
Tobar na h-Òige 77
Tobar nan Clèireach 77
Toberdonich 54
Tolm, An 78
Tom na h-Iùbhraich 6, 31, 32, 87
Tom nan Ceann 33, 54
Tòmas an Tòdhair 26
Tomnahurich 6, 31, 32, 44, 87
Torbreck 88
Tòrr Mòr, An 54
Torvean 17, 84, 88
Travelling people 53
Tucker, Thomas 20

Watson, William J 44, 57, 69, 74, 78, 81, 86
Well of the Spotted Rock 48
Well of the Washing Burn see Fuaran Allt an
                                    Ionnlaid
Wells, Culloden 77
Witches 21